MANGE.
PSALM 139

Death to Life

Micah MacDonald

DEATH TO LIFE

CONTENTS

ACKNOWLEDGEMENTS

This book wouldn't have been possible without the love and saving grace of Jesus. He is a Father to the fatherless, and I know Him as such. I have experienced His promises firsthand. Psalm 34 says to "taste and see that the Lord is good." I have encountered God's goodness over and over again. Apart from Jesus, I can do nothing.

Steph: It is because of Christ that my steps have been ordered, which include the blessing of finding my wife. You have watched this story play out firsthand. I remember introducing you to my youth pastor, Ryan Skoog. He pulled me aside in his kitchen and said, "Micah, you experienced one of the greatest losses in your life in losing your dad. However, God gave you one of the greatest joys in your life by giving you Steph." I consider it a joy each and every day to do life with the best teammate and partner on the earth. I can't believe I got you. If anyone needs proof that God still does miracles today, you can just look at me and then look at Steph. You will see that I don't deserve this lady. Ha ha.

Truly, to have you by my side through the worst moments and through the best has been incredible. Thank you for your love, constant support and encouragement to go after Jesus first.

Everleigh and Malachi: You cannot read or understand what I am writing in this book, as you just turned four and two years old. But what I think is so cool about this book is that, one day, you'll get to hear the story of God's faithfulness over our family and our lives. I have always said in my preaching that one day these children and future grandchildren of mine will be able to hear the story of God's goodness in the middle of brokenness. One of my prayers for you kids is that you and the future generations of the MacDonald family line will serve and love Jesus with all of your hearts! Jesus is worth it all. JESUS IS WORTHY. Kids, I love you and am so proud of you.

Pastor Jerry: God placed you in our lives for a major purpose. I often think of you and Kathy and your leadership as a crucial part of my own personal and spiritual development. You were obedient to God during key moments in my life. You helped pastor and shepherd me at times when I was the most vulnerable and hurting. You led me and continue to be a voice of encouragement in my life. Thank you for pastoring me and being obedient to Jesus.

Ryan Skoog and Chris Book: Thank you for youth pastoring me and teaching me how to pray and have bold faith. Thank you for correcting me and loving me enough to speak the truth in love. Thank you for being an example and loving students. You showed me how to do that by the way you live your lives. Chris, it was your love for middle school students that got a hold of my life. You asked me to go on my first ever mission trip and it changed my life forever. Ryan, you taught me how to pray. You taught me how to pray in the Spirit and how to follow Jesus' voice.

Jeremy Chapman, Andrew Johnston, Brent Silkey, Josiah Kennealy:

Jeremy, thanks for letting me come over to your house after church on Sundays and for giving me a safe place to grow as an intern and leader. Thanks for modeling a love for Christ and your family and the role of a father in your own home. It spoke and ministered to me.

Andrew, thank you for being the God-given voice that didn't let me quit when I felt like quitting in ministry. Thank you for looking me in the eye and speaking truth over me when I was believing a lie. Thank you for your leadership and stewardship over the things you saw in my life. I love you so much.

Brent. thanks for being a catalyst in my life. Thank you for spurring me on in greater faith for the impossible. Thanks for holding me up when I couldn't walk, literally and spiritually, whether it was carrying me through a full Twin Cities marathon or holding me up in the hospital when my dad passed away. Brent, God has used you instrumentally to be a best friend for me. Thank you.

Josiah, when I am having a bad day, I just want to call and talk to you. I have so appreciated your friendship and encouragement over the years. You and Micah are a gift to our home and family. I have appreciated the bro trips and look forward to more.

Chris Rausch and Rausch Family:

You have been with me from the beginning. I am

convinced that when God says He places the lonely in families, He handpicked your family for a lonely young man who would do whatever he could to stay as long as he could in the Rausch home. I find myself easily moved to tears when I think of the role your family and friendship has played in my life and development. Thank you for loving on me and treating me as one of your own.

Chris, it has been so fun to see our lives move forward together, whether we were miles apart or within a few miles of one another. God knew I needed a friend like you. Thank you for challenging me, walking with me, and being present through it all. I love you, man.

Mom: Thank you. Thank you for showing me what grit and faith look like. The best decision you ever made was prioritizing faith in Christ and finding a church that would allow us to grow with other followers of Jesus. You are a hero to me.

Brittany, Jacqueline, Victoria: Wow. I wouldn't have wanted to journey this life with any other siblings. I love each of you and am so proud of the women you have become. I understand your journeys have been different than mine, but what has been the common theme is God's faithfulness. Thank you for being sisters who love and speak life! I can't wait to see God's promises unfold in each of your lives as we keep following Him.

Dad: I miss you. I love you. I know how proud you would have been of your grandkids Ev and Malachi. I often think of you and wish you were still here. Thanks for loving me and leading me in the way of Jesus. I remember the best things about you, and I choose to hold onto the way God saw you and made you.

I could write for hours about other people and the role Cedar Valley Church has played within my life. However, I can't spend the rest of the time doing that or else we would have another book. Nevertheless, thank you. Thank you for picking up this book and playing a part in the story God has given us.

TO GOD BE THE GLORY FOREVER AND EVER. AMEN.

Foreword

The day Micah showed up halfway into my New Testament class (which he was NOT enrolled in) at North Central University with a Green Machine Naked Juice, a loaf of white Wonder Bread, and the tub of Kraft peanut butter he'd stolen from me the week before was the day I knew Micah was special. I mean, who does that? Micah Mac does. Just like that day he entered the classroom 25 minutes late to my 50-minute class, Micah is willing to push past every boundary and blow up every "norm" for the sake of reaching the one. Micah is passion-filled, generous with his friendships, and loves deeply. Not only that but he always brings the fun. And who ever said Christians can't be fun?

Micah has a deep desire to continue to learn and grow. After all, leaders are learners, and learners always grow. Throughout the 11 years that I've known Micah, and especially in the time that I've been his wife, I have seen his love for Jesus and His Church do nothing but grow. Through every season, even the more challenging ones, I've seen Micah lean into Scripture and prayer. And I've seen good fruit come from it—like the kind of fruit John 15 talks about. I have watched him remain tender toward correction and tough toward ridicule, always asking himself, "What can I learn from this?"

Nothing will stop what Micah sets his mind to. So, when Micah said he wanted to write a book, I knew it was just a matter of time before I would be able to hold a copy in my hands and page through many of the stories I've heard him share from the stage—and seen him live out offstage as a father, husband, friend, and ministry leader.

This book is filled with stories of God's faithfulness, power and hope. I trust and pray that it will encourage you, that you will remember Jesus above all else, and that there will be an area in your life where you see Jesus bring it "from death to life."

Let's go!

DEATH TO LIFE

INTRODUCTION

I remember sitting in the hospital room after my newborn baby girl entered the world. I was witnessing life in its purest form. Someone who had never taken her first breath outside the womb was now in my arms and breathing on her own.

As I held Everleigh Dawn, I broke down and cried. I wept and prayed over my daughter. I prayed over her future. I prophesied over her life as the Spirit enabled me. I thanked God for the gift of life.

Hours later it hit me. My father had passed away from a motorcycle accident in the same hospital where my daughter was just born. I'd watched as Dad lay lifeless from a brain injury and experienced the pains of death. Have you ever lost a loved one? Have you ever witnessed death? It can be traumatic and have many emotions attached to it.

The concept of life is unbelievable when I think about it. We are all guaranteed one thing: death. However, before we ever experience death, we first are born. We first are given life before we experience death. As I held my daughter, I couldn't help thinking of my father dying in the same exact hospital. Then I thought about our relationship with God.

Scripture tells us that we are all born sinners and that the wages of sin is death. Apart from Jesus, we are dead. We are dead in our sins and dead in our own transgressions. When we encounter Christ, we experience a beautiful journey from death to life. We experience His power and saving grace that take us from a place of being dead in our sins to alive in Him. We get to receive His resurrection power, going from places of death to places of life. I witnessed death firsthand with my father and, years later, witnessed life in the birth of my brand-new daughter. It is such a crazy concept to wrap our minds around, but the longer we follow Jesus the more we realize that He is all about raising the dead parts of us back to LIFE.

This book is only possible because of the promises in Scripture and because I serve a God who is true to His Word and promises. I would love for you to journey with me in watching a story unfold from moments of death to moments of life, a story that only God could write. Not only did He do all of this for me, but His promises in His Word apply to you too!

Chapter 1

When Storms Hit

I am the oldest in my family, and I have three younger sisters. If you are a man reading this and you grew up with all sisters, you either have anger issues, or you are the gentlest, most patient, loving, and understanding human being aside from Jesus Himself. Kidding, but serious.

I was honored to be the big brother in our household, but the role came with its challenges when I wanted to reenact Lion King. I was Simba while my sisters played Scar. I could never fully interact and wrestle with my sisters, because it would end in a screaming match. Then they would run crying to Mom, tell her I'd hurt them, and that ruined all the fun.

So, I succumbed and joined in their fun. I was the "Easy-Bake Oven" guy and had to wear an apron. (Just Google "Easy-Bake Oven." Brilliant creation.) There were times when my sisters would dress me up, put makeup on me, then take pictures. How did I get the short end of the stick? I still don't know, and I'm still working through issues today. Ha ha. However, when I look back on being the oldest, I count it a joy and privilege to walk alongside my sisters and family.

Having three sisters helped me form a special relationship with my father, who was DIFFERENT. Dad was unique and special. He had the ability to walk into any room and make it fun and exciting. From when I was an infant to 12 years old, I learned what it meant to be a man, a husband, and a father by watching my dad. He was a hard worker. He was a volunteer fire fighter and always told the most riveting near-death experiences. Dad was also a part-time youth pastor and a pest control employee. (He was so successful at it that he eventually started his own company.)

My father and I shared a passion for sports. Some of my favorite memories of my dad are from when all my buddies would come over and play sports in our backyard for hours. We would play football, soccer, baseball and basketball, and Dad wouldn't just stay in the house. He couldn't resist coming out to play with me and my friends and being "all-time QB", the pitcher, or another position depending on the sport. We always had so much fun but, at the same time, it was kind of annoying ...

My dad loved my mom. I looked forward to when they would go on dates, because it meant a fun babysitter was coming over and we'd build forts and have the best of times. Once a month my dad would take each of us kids out individually on a "date" to get an ice cream cone or just to tell us how much he loved us. He had a way of winning us over with laughter and charisma. When Dad was around. we could be ourselves and knew everything was going to be okay.

My father was my hero. If someone asked me who I wanted to be like, I would answer, "My dad." I saw the way he loved Jesus and others, and I wanted to be just like him. The times we had together were special and I will never forget them. Moments that stand out in particular are from when we'd go to the rink at the local park in the winter and play pickup hockey for a couple of hours. We went inside for occasional breaks to warm up our toes and drink hot chocolate. However, what I remember most about those nights is my dad witnessing and sharing his faith in Jesus with all of the young hockey players out on the ice. My dad showed me that his faith in Jesus was real and genuine, so much so that he couldn't stay quiet about Him. My dad prayed with those guys to receive Christ, and it left me wanting to do the same thing.

I would go into the living room or my parents' bedroom in the mornings and see my dad with his coffee and his Bible. I remember him coming home from mission trips and excitedly sharing stories about what God had done through the mission team and people they ministered to. His passion for Jesus was real and contagious!

Other times engrained in my mind are from when the youth group would meet in the basement of our house. My dad was a youth pastor for a church plant. I remember creeping down the stairs to spy on the meeting and hearing worship music and seeing young people crying out to Jesus. I remember the sincere prayers, tears, and emotion they had as they encountered Christ. I so badly wanted to be a part of the youth group, but my dad always told me I needed to wait a couple more years before I could join.

Well, I hit the age when I could finally join the youth group, but there was one problem. The youth group wasn't meeting anymore. The church had dissolved due to a transition in leadership, and my dad then transitioned away from ministry. Something different began happening in our home. Subtle changes took place before my very eyes. I watched my dad gradually change as the months passed. The music in our house began to shift. My dad's lifestyle began to change. Arguments between my mom and dad started to arise.

Everyday life was changing. It got real whenever I heard my mother crying from across the hallway. There were countless nights when I'd sit at the end of her bed not knowing what to say or how to comfort her. I would ask what was causing her so much heartache, but she never opened up to me.

At the age of 12, I was smart enough to notice that my dad wasn't in bed next to her. He would come home from the bar late at night, smelling like smoke and stumbling around drunk. Hard liquor, alcohol, drugs, and smoking became normal for my dad. Rather than seeing him with his Bible open and spending time with Jesus, I'd find him doing hard drugs, which he tried to hide from me. He'd say, "Hey, buddy, why don't you watch the game in the other room? I'll be there in a moment." My sisters were too young to realize what was happening at the time, but I was watching my hero choose a different life. The fights began to intensify. Once when my parents were arguing, it got so intense that my mom called the police and my dad ripped the phone cord out of the wall. I saw him get arrested in our home that day. I had never seen him in handcuffs. I can still hear the cries of my sisters not wanting Dad to leave the house. He was taken to jail that night, and our home was being torn in two.

As a young man, I saw things that I never should have had to see. My dad cheated on my mom with other women. I watched as the drugs and lifestyle choices that broke my heart continued in my dad's life. All of it led to a moment in our living room that I will never forget.

It was a normal afternoon until my parents called a family meeting. My dad sat all of us kids down and explained that he would be divorcing my mom. My mom looked at my dad and said, "Tell them, Chuck. Tell them what else." The tension in the room was thick, and my sisters and I held onto every word that was coming out of our father's mouth. As he spoke about divorce, I could see the fear, panic and "what does this mean for us now?" on my sisters' faces. Our parents had been married for 17 years and it was ending. I was at a loss for words and didn't know where to turn. I'd just experienced my hero walking out the door. In a moment, I became the man of the house and the older male figure for my younger sisters. I began to fill a role that was never mine to fill, and it forever changed me.

I've heard it said that every person is either about to go through a storm, currently in a storm, or coming out of a storm. I have seen families who have great lives, love Jesus, and have minimal issues. Quite often those same families eventually reach out saying, "Dad now has a heart condition," or "Mom has issues with her memory" or someone is unable to get pregnant or had a miscarriage. In life, it's not a matter of if you will go through a storm but when you will go through one. The storm we were going through seemed more like death, and the thought of life seemed far off. Our lives now included awkward family gatherings, trying to get used to living in a different house every other weekend, and sometimes feeling trapped in between two different worlds.

There was Mom's house and Dad's house. My sisters and I were left to navigate life with both a single father and a single mother trying to parent us. I broke for my dad when he attempted to cook for us, because that was something Mom always did. I broke for my mom who was trying to raise us alone. She went back to school and tried to get a degree because she'd never gone to college. She worked multiple jobs to provide for us.

It seemed as though Mom and Dad were still arguing over money even though they were divorced. I almost never asked for money. I tried to get a job as soon as I could. I knew money was tight and that if I wanted something, I would need to work to pay for it myself. I can recall hearing my mother wondering out loud if child support was going to come in on time or if my dad would make his payment late again. She would openly share her fear that she might not be able to make the mortgage payment. We all began to worry, not knowing what would happen next.

Have you ever found yourself in a storm where the pain ran so deep that you began to say, "God, where are you?" or "Why didn't you show up when I needed you the most?" In life, it's easy to have more questions than answers. You know the saying: "Time heals all wounds." Well, we were wondering when our time would come. We wanted to know when we would catch a break. But things never got better. They actually got worse, and the pain only grew deeper. The storm was only beginning, and another element had just made it worse.

Chapter 2

The Absence of Jesus

Has the storm ever gotten so bad that you couldn't see Jesus anymore? Have you ever said, "Jesus, where are you?" or "Why didn't you show up when I needed you most?" That question makes me think of one story in particular.

A young man and his two sisters were raised in a typical home, but things began to shift when they encountered Jesus. Even the dynamic of their relationship as siblings changed. Isn't it funny how quickly transformative Jesus' love can be? Anyway, faith in Jesus became very real for all three of the siblings. It was no longer just their parents' faith; it became personal to them.

One day the brother described to his sisters how he had been feeling sick and that his symptoms were getting worse, and they encouraged him to see a doctor. The brother refused, as he was stubborn and didn't like doctors. However, he started feeling badly enough that he eventually decided to go. After taking a variety of tests with the nurses, the doctor came into the room to speak with him.

The doctor looked at the young man and said, "Son, do you have family?" He responded, "Yeah, I do. But why does that matter?" Then the doctor dropped a statement that would forever change the young man's life. He said, "Son, I am sorry to tell you this, but you have a terminal disease and there is no medical cure. You have maybe a few months left to live, and you are going to need your family around you during this difficult time. I am so sorry to have to tell you this, but you need to get home and let your family know." The young man began to freak out. He questioned the doctor and didn't believe that what he'd heard was true, but the doctor helped him calm down and encouraged him to go home and tell his family.

When the young man got home, he gathered his family around the dining room table and, through tears, told them the news that he had only a few months to live. His family broke down and immediately surrounded him. After a long while of holding each other and crying, the sisters began to speak up. They spoke about knowing

Jesus and that He could heal. They had seen Him heal before, and they knew He could do it again. They assured their brother that he would be okay, because Jesus would show up and perform another miracle.

The sisters' faith was sky high and they went to drastic measures calling on Jesus to heal their brother. They hosted prayer meetings day and night, believing their brother would be healed in the name of Jesus. Their faith was unwavering, immovable and unshakeable. They were not going to stop praying until they saw a miracle. Day after day went by and, instead of their brother getting better, his condition only got worse. But the sisters didn't get discouraged.

The doctor later updated the family, saying, "He has only about a week left to live." He encouraged the family to reach out to loved ones and have them stop by the house to say their final prayers and goodbyes. The sisters heard this and, rather than growing weak, they became that much more persistent in prayer and in their belief that Jesus would heal their brother.

One evening, as the family was around the young man's

bed, they witnessed the worst outcome possible. They watched as he struggled and gasped for air and took his final breath on Earth. The sisters screamed and yelled. They had just experienced the greatest loss of their life. The tears wouldn't stop, and they were filled with anger and resentment. After crying for a while, they began to speak.

"JESUS, IF YOU WOULD HAVE JUST SHOWN UP, OUR BROTHER WOULDN'T HAVE DIED. JESUS, IF YOU WOULD HAVE JUST BEEN HERE WHEN WE ASKED YOU TO COME, OUR BROTHER NEVER WOULD HAVE DIED."

This. This right here is the tension in the human life and human heart. What happens when your current realities don't line up with the character of God? What happens when Jesus doesn't show up the way you expect and want Him to? What happens when everything around you is so painful and dark that all you can say is, "JESUS, WHERE ARE YOU? WHY DIDN'T YOU SHOW UP WHEN I ASKED?"

Have you ever been there before?

The story I just shared happens to be a modern-day version of a story found in the Bible involving a brother named Lazarus and two sisters named Mary and Martha.

Lazarus, Mary and Martha were all very good friends with Jesus. They had spent time with Jesus and witnessed His ministry up close and personal. Mary and Martha knew that Jesus was a miracle worker, and they had all the confidence in the world that Jesus would surely come through and heal their brother, Lazarus. Instead of showing up when they called out to Him, Jesus showed up after Lazarus died.

I'm not sure if you can relate at all to Mary and Martha, but I know I can.

I thought the storm was coming to an end after my parents' divorce, but I didn't realize it was only just getting started. One night, a year after my parents split, my mom was tucking my youngest sister in bed and scratching her back like moms do. (By the way, back scratches from Mom are the best, y'all.) While she was scratching her back, my mother also came across a big bump on my sister's leg. My mom asked her, "Victoria, what is this bump on your leg?" Victoria replied, "Oh, it's just a bruise, Mom." My mother knew it wasn't just a bruise, so she set up an appointment to take her to the doctor.

At the appointment, the doctor recommended scans to find out what was in Victoria's leg. Once we received the results, we found out that my eight-year-old sister had a six-inch by eight-inch tumor wrapped around her femur, also known as the thighbone. After a biopsy to learn how severe the tumor was, we discovered that Victoria had stage four synovial cell sarcoma cancer. The doctor gave her about a twenty percent chance to live because we'd found out about it so late.

I'd just watched my mom and dad divorce a year before, and then I got the news that my youngest sister had a twenty percent chance to live. I started thinking and said, "JESUS, IF YOU WOULD HAVE JUST SHOWN UP, MY DAD WOULDN'T HAVE LEFT. JESUS, IF YOU WOULD HAVE JUST SHOWN UP, MY SISTER NEVER WOULD HAVE HAD CANCER." I wonder how many times each of us has thought similar words. "Jesus, if you would have just shown up, I would have never been abused. Jesus, if you would have just shown up, I never would have had to go through this divorce. Jesus, if you would have just shown up, I never would have had to be a single mom. Jesus, if you would have just shown up, I never would have had this disease." You fill in the blank.

When the storm gets closer or harder to endure, we can feel like Jesus is absent. Is God still good through all of this? Where is He? Why isn't He showing up when I want Him to show up? Why didn't He come when I prayed and asked Him to? Too often I have related to how Mary and Martha must have felt in the story found in John 11.

The response Jesus gives in John 11:4 when He finds out His really good friend Lazarus is sick gives us more insight into how He works more often than not. Jesus hears the news that His buddy is sick, and His response is POWERFUL. The Bible says, "When he heard this, Jesus said, 'This sickness will not end in death. No, it is for God's glory so that God's Son may be glorified through it.'"

This verse is key for us to understand everything about

LIFE. When we're hit with hard circumstances, we don't often remember that God has a plan through it all. Our natural response is to focus on the storm and forget the one who holds everything in His hands. How often do we forget that everything we are is for God's glory and not ours? Maybe, just maybe, if we actually trusted God and waited on Him, we might see Jesus get a whole lot of glory from our lives and circumstances. Jesus said the sickness Lazarus had wouldn't end in death but would be for God's glory so that Jesus would be glorified.

Many of us quit before we ever see the full effect of God's glory being worked out in our lives. We stop when the storm comes, because we see the big storm versus our bigger God and His MASTER PLAN. Jesus had a plan that Mary and Martha couldn't see. You and I can easily forget that even when we experience the sting of death or when bad things happen, God wastes nothing. He takes everything about our lives and uses it for His good and His glory. He can work powerfully in a moment, but He can change the world through a LIFETIME of obedience and TRUST.

When fear comes crashing in and we get the unexpected news that we dread, a couple of scenarios can play out.

The first act of defense is usually to self-protect or to try and gain control. This may be a natural initial reaction to a traumatic event, but it shouldn't be long lasting. When we look at Scripture, we see a greater narrative at play. We see a heavenly Father who gave us His Holy Spirit and who wants us to let go and trust Him to take the lead.

We often do more damage to ourselves and others when we attempt to control everything. Our desire to be in control is one of the reasons we all try to self-medicate, find solutions to our pain, or get through something. It's why we turn to drugs, alcohol, pornography, or any other addictive behaviors. We start off with an idea to numb or protect ourselves from the issues at hand. But if we press play on the movie with the decision to participate in destructive ways, we'll wind up causing devastation to ourselves and those closest to us.

All along Jesus has said, "If you would just trust me and let me lead your life, you will watch how I work for your good and the good of others around you. You will watch how I get glory through all of this."

Mary and Martha struggled to see what Jesus was getting at, because their reality wasn't a brother who was healed but a brother who was dead—and who had been dead for four days when Jesus decided to show up. In their minds, the absence of Jesus equated to a dead brother. Nevertheless, what Jesus saw wasn't a dead brother but a perfectly timed demonstration of His power.

I don't understand the timing of Jesus; I probably never will. But one thing I do know is that when Jesus shows up, He changes everything.

Chapter 3

Jesus Gets the Final Word

The power of words is incredible. Words have the ability to do permanent damage or bring permanent healing. I can remember a time when I was hanging out with a bunch of my friends after we'd just finished playing a classic "Shirts vs. Skins" game of basketball. I was self-conscious about taking my shirt off, but what made it ten times worse was when one of my friends looked at me and said, "Hey, everyone, look! It's Rolley!" He was referring to the rolls on my stomach, and it just about made me scream and run away. I was already insecure, and now my friends were pointing out an insecurity.

Those words hurt me. Words have the ability to hurt and they also have the ability to heal. Some of our greatest wounds are often caused by the most hurt-filled words. I think of moms and dads who have verbally abused their kids. I think of how many people are picked on, bullied, or made fun of virtually or face-to-face. The world is full of hurtful words. However, Jesus spoke some of the most powerful words ever—words that have changed history as we know it. When He was hanging on a cross, naked, beaten and bleeding, He cried out, "Father, forgive them." Even up until some of His final breaths, the Savior of the world was uttering FORGIVENESS.

Behind every word is a meaning and motive. Jesus' words were demonstrations of His character. Throughout His life, the words He used were meant to heal, convict, forgive, restore, and build others up. His words were filled with purpose. He stood up for the widows, poor, lame, blind, fatherless, and for all of the injustices in His time. His words came across as offensive to those who needed to be challenged.

Before you take in someone's words, you need to evaluate and weigh them. Good questions to ask yourself when someone speaks to you are:

1. Does this person know me?
2. Do I have a relationship with this person?
3. Is there truth to what this person is saying?
4. Is this person trustworthy, someone with integrity and good character?

There are more ways to filter others' words that I could mention, but the words you can always count on are the words Jesus speaks. When Jesus says something, you can believe and trust in it wholeheartedly.

Jesus had some words to say when He intentionally showed up late to visit Mary, Martha and Lazarus. Before He could say anything, Martha ran out to give Him a mouthful of her own. The first words she said were, "Lord, if you would have been here, my brother would not have died." Martha held nothing back. She went for the knockout punch right away. I can imagine the frustration and anger she and Mary were experiencing. They'd just lost their brother, and a big reason why was because this man named Jesus decided not to come when they wanted Him to come. They knew Jesus had all the power to perform a miracle for their brother. I love the honesty Martha showed in baring her heart to Him.

Before I continue, I want to make a quick note of something. Jesus wants your honesty. He wants your anger, frustration, and questions. Jesus can handle it. He doesn't want a fake you; He wants a real you. I want to challenge you to be honest with God. Be honest with

Him about the details of your life. A great way to do this is to spend time in prayer. Shout, scream, cry, or write any or all of your thoughts.

Martha got brutally honest with Jesus, but He responded with words that cut right through it all. Jesus looked her in the eyes and said, "Martha, your brother will rise again." Jesus addressed Martha about an issue from the past. Jesus spoke about the death of her brother, which had taken place four days before. I just want to make something very clear: Jesus always gets the FINAL WORD ABOUT YOUR PAST.

This is a word for somebody right now. Martha and Mary were dwelling on the past. The loss of a loved one and the grief associated with that will be a process until the day you die. But Jesus spoke to Martha about a past situation and told her that her brother would rise again. The words Jesus responded with were powerful. Even Martha didn't think He meant "right now" but in the last days. Martha wasn't tracking with Jesus. In the same way, He uses His words to bring healing concerning issues from our own pasts. So, why is it that many of us continue to live with the pain of our old wounds?

I have found that one of Satan's greatest tactics in the lives of those who follow Christ is to bring up our pasts in an effort to shame us, keeping us locked up and far from Jesus. There are countless followers of Jesus who never taste and experience true freedom because of the shame of past events, which is designed to keep us in chains and far from Him.

If Jesus isn't dwelling on the past, then why do we spend so much time dwelling on it? You and I aren't meant to live staring into a rearview mirror but looking forward toward the eternal prize that awaits us. Psalm 103 speaks about how God lifts us up from the pit and puts a crown on our heads. Verses 11-12 say, "For as high as the heavens are above the earth, so great is his love for those who fear him; as far as the east is from the west; so far has he removed our transgressions from us." That's some good news right there!

The reason the devil is always bringing up your past is because he has no future. He has already been defeated by the victory Christ won through His death and resurrection. Sin, death and destruction no longer have any power over your life. Romans 6:6-7 says, "For we know that our old self was crucified with him so that the body ruled by sin might be done away with, that we should no longer be slaves to sin—because anyone who has died has been set free from sin." Romans 6:11-12 says, "In the same way, count yourselves dead to sin but alive to God in Christ Jesus. Therefore, do not let sin reign in your mortal body so that you obey its evil desires."

Shame has the ability to alter your reality and push you into false living. Shame says that you are unworthy of the love of Christ. Shame says that what happened in your past will always be the truest thing about you. Jesus didn't come so you could stay in shame. He came with all authority and power to cut right through the shame and bring words of LIFE and FREEDOM.

The question is: Do you believe this? Jesus looked at Martha after He said that her brother would rise again, and He made a BOLD statement. In John 11:25, Jesus says, "I am the resurrection and the life. The one who believes in me will live, even though they die; and whoever lives by believing in me will never die. Do you believe this?" Jesus was infusing hope into a hopeless situation. He got the final word about a situation that occurred in the past, and He STILL gets the final word about *your* past.

If there was anyone who had a rough history, it was a guy named Saul. He was known for accusing the early Christ followers, and he saw it as his personal mission to murder and terrorize those who believed in Jesus. In Acts 7, we learn about a man named Stephen who was stoned to death for declaring the gospel and the truth about Jesus. The people who executed Stephen took off their coats and laid them at the feet of Saul, who went on to witness the deaths of numerous followers of Jesus. If there was anyone who was too far out of reach for the love of Jesus, you could make the case that it was Saul.

One day, everything changed while Saul was traveling and encountered Christ for himself. Saul went from being a terrorist to a full-blown believer and follower of Jesus. He had seen the glory and majesty of King Jesus with his own eyes. How could someone who was incredibly passionate, zealous and firm in his beliefs suddenly change overnight? I have seen this play out right before my eyes with drug dealers, broken families, prostitutes, you name it. The love of Jesus transformed them all in an instant.

Sometime after Saul began to follow Jesus, he became known as Paul. He wrote a powerful passage in Philippians 3, where he speaks about his life and resumé. Paul mentioned that everything he'd gained in his life was utterly meaningless in comparison to knowing Christ and His love. He then went on to write about his new ambitions. In verses 12-14, he says, "Not that I have already obtained all this, or have already arrived at my goal, but I press on to take hold of that for which Christ Jesus took hold of me. Brothers and sisters, I do not consider myself yet to have taken hold of it. But one thing I do: Forgetting what is behind and straining toward what is ahead, I press on toward the goal to win the prize for which God has called me heavenward in Christ Jesus."

Paul knew it was draining and a waste of Jesus' grace and mercy to focus on his past. He believed that it was essential to FORGET THE PAST and to gaze ahead. Jesus' words that day were enough for Paul to recognize that He gets the final word about his past.

I think about my own life, the mistakes, sin, pressures, temptations, and the evil I experienced. When people listen to my story, they don't expect to hear the outcome I share with them. If it weren't for Jesus finding me as a broken, hurting young man, I don't know where I would be today. If it weren't for Jesus getting the final word about my life, I would be in a very dark place. There is no difference between you and me. If Jesus could ask you a question, He would say, "I am the way, the truth, and the life. Do you believe this?" To believe in Jesus is to surrender your mind and entire life to Him. The old way of living shifts to a new way of living. The old life is gone, and a new life begins.

Martha had yet to realize the full weight of Jesus' words, but He was surely about to blow her mind. When He speaks, He means and does what He says. His words will never fail or let you down, and they will always move you from a place of death to a place of life. Jesus always gets the final word about your past.

Chapter 4

I'm Right Here

I remember who I called first on the day my parents sat us kids down in the living room to tell us they were getting a divorce. After they broke the news, the tears began rolling down my sisters' cheeks, as we were all hit with the uncertainty that lay ahead of us. A numb look came across my mother's face. I know she was trying to be strong for the four kids she was about to lead into uncharted territory. The pain was so real and so heavy.

I went to my bedroom and called my best friend. "Chris, my parents are getting a divorce." His immediate response was, "I'll be right there. My dad and I are coming over right now." There's something comforting about knowing you aren't alone and that someone is right there with you. Throughout my life, Chris has been a friend who has always been there. He didn't say many words, but his presence and his family, who took me in as their own, communicated to me, "We're right here."

The Rausch family became a beacon of hope for me. Dave and Lois took me into their home when I was hurting and broken. Their house became a safe place, a refuge where I could come as I was and heal. I felt so safe at their house that on multiple nights I tried to hide in Chris' bedroom so I could spend the night. Their family brought stability to me while my family was shaking. I remember family dinners and laughing so hard. I remember basketball games in the backyard and playing video games for hours. The Rausch family even took me on my first ever plane ride and vacation to San Antonio. I always wanted to have brothers growing up but, since I had three sisters, I obviously thought that would never be a reality. However, Chris and his two younger brothers quickly became my brothers, too.

In the summertime, we'd go up to their farm and shoot guns, hit golf balls over the road, and simply be at peace with life. Their family provided something for me that every young person needs: security. They never had to use their words to tell me, but if one thing was clear about them, it was that they were communicating, "Micah, we are right here."

Oftentimes, when people go through their greatest

suffering, they don't need more sermons and long speeches. They just need someone to sit in the pain with them long enough for them to heal. Words usually don't cut it when it comes to loss and heartache, but if someone is willing to come over and cry with you, now that's a different story.

Loneliness is crippling our world. We have instant connection at our fingertips but truly lack intimacy with friends, loved ones and others. We are content with letting people stay within an arm's length of us but on the inside, we may be crumbling. In the very beginning, even God noticed it wasn't good for man to be alone; therefore, He created woman to be a helper and suiter for the man. From the start, it has been God's plan that we would never live in isolation but that His creation would know intimacy through relationship with one another. My heart breaks to see people walk through life in loneliness, and I know it doesn't just break my heart. It also breaks the heart of God. You and I were always meant to do life together and never alone. Jesus modeled this from the get-go when He chose to minister alongside disciples who would be with Him everywhere He went. Jesus was setting the example for what the kingdom of heaven on Earth would look like, and it always involved togetherness—even under the worst and most painful circumstances. When we read John 11 and see Mary and Martha mourning, we can sometimes forget that Jesus felt the pain just as much. He was fully God and fully man, which means He endured and felt every human emotion that Mary and Martha did. Jesus had lost someone He loved, too.

After Jesus finishes talking to Martha, the next person we see come on the scene is Mary. John 11:32 says, "When Mary reached the place where Jesus was and saw him, she fell at his feet and said, 'Lord if you would have been here, my brother would not have died.'" Mary said the exact words Martha had moments before. The narrative in their hearts was the same: "Jesus, you didn't show up when we needed you." Every time you see Mary mentioned in Scripture, you see her at the feet of Jesus. I want to direct your attention to the posture she always took when she saw Jesus. In those days, Jews did not bow down to anyone except God. Mary was constantly found at Jesus' feet. To bow at a rabbi's feet meant you were in submission to a rabbi and his teaching. Women would never bow down at a rabbi's feet, as that was a practice reserved for men who were a rabbi's disciples. In an earlier story, Jesus commended Mary for sitting at His feet, and Martha was challenged to do the same. I am convinced that the only way to thrive in life is to live in what Jesus has wanted all along: relationship.

When Mary placed herself at the feet of Jesus, what she was communicating to Him was, "I AM RIGHT HERE. I AM ALL YOURS. YOU HAVE MY UNDIVIDED ATTENTION. I WILLINGLY PLACE MYSELF BEFORE YOU." This posture will always move the heart of Jesus. It's what He wants most. In John 15, He told His disciples to abide with Him and remain in His love, so that their fruit might abound in their lives.

Mary was crushed with grief. She was sad, angry, and full of other emotions. Wherever you find yourself, you will never lack any good thing when you place your heart and life at the feet of Jesus. This isn't just good self-talk. This is a promise found in Scripture, as the book of Psalm speaks about how man lacks no good thing when he seeks God.

When storms come, the problem is that we do everything else besides throw ourselves at Jesus' feet. We attempt to take life into our own hands. We try to live behind the masks of our own making. We hide behind the medicine, pain killers, and thousands of dollars spent on ourselves, yet we never feel satisfied or whole. We tell ourselves that time heals all wounds. In reality, wounds won't heal through time, but they will always heal through Jesus.

Mary chose the better thing, the hard thing. She chose again to find herself at the feet of Jesus. She communicated a message to Him: "I am broken. I am hurting, and I am right here." I love what happened to Jesus when He saw Mary in her brokenness. John 11:33-35 says, "When Jesus saw her weeping, and the Jews who had come along with her also weeping, he was deeply moved in spirit and troubled. 'Where have you laid him?' He asked. 'Come and see, Lord,' they replied. JESUS WEPT." In this moment, we get one of the all-time most beautiful pictures in Scripture on the full humanity of Jesus. When Jesus encounters brokenness, He doesn't burst into song or a full-out sermon. You never see Jesus tell people to sit down and listen to His eloquent speech. Rather, in the middle of the weeping, it says that Jesus wept.

Stop for a second. Please, don't bypass this. Stop and picture the Savior of the world weeping along with those who are weeping. Great emotion comes in the middle of great pain. Have you ever cried uncontrollably—just ugly cried? That is exactly what happened in that moment. Hebrews 4:15 says, "For we do not have a high priest who is unable to empathize with our weaknesses, but we have one who has been tempted in every way, just as we are—yet he did not sin." Jesus understands empathy and compassion. We serve a God who understands the human mind, emotion and will. The response that Jesus gives is so moving. He mourns with those who mourn. He comforts those who need comforting. He weeps with those who weep. I can relate with this in a crazy way.

Things got very bad after my parents' divorce. There was ongoing drama between my mom and dad, and I felt caught in the middle of two different worlds. I was trying to be strong for my mom and sisters yet trying to understand my dad. I recall my sisters and I sitting down in his living room to tell him that we didn't want to see him until he gave up the drugs and hard liquor among other things. Dad didn't take it well. He erupted, saying he was going to live his life however he wanted and would never step foot inside of church ever again. After that night, there was a period of about three years when we didn't talk to or see him. Those three years were very confusing to me and my sisters. We were young and wanted our dad back in our lives the way we'd known him.

To make a long story short. a motorcycle accident that almost took Dad's life is what brought us back together. His body hit a road sign and he ended up in a ditch. A young man helped turn his body upside down so the bleeding in his leg would be elevated above his heart. The doctors ended up having to amputate his leg above the knee to save his life. When I stepped into the hospital room, his head looked like a balloon due to the swelling. He was heavily sedated, and I said, "Dad, it's us and the kids." He couldn't respond to us with words, but he did through his tears. He began to cry when he heard our voices, which is a moment I will never forget. Three years of not seeing our dad was coming to an end, and we were starting the journey back to relationship. I remember him saying, "Kids, had I known it would take losing my leg to see you guys again, I would have given up my leg a long time ago." He'd held onto all of our Christmas presents and birthday gifts over those three years. It was difficult and emotional for my sisters and I to restore our relationship with him, and each of us had a different path. However, there were a couple of even more difficult moments that will mark me forever.

One of my dreams as a boy was to one day preach with my dad. I'd watched him preach the word of God, and I was always inspired by him. My father was a gifted communicator and could move audiences in a powerful way. One day, he called, saying, "Hey, kids, you want to go to church with me?" I remember thinking to myself, "Dad, is that you?" That Sunday morning, we pulled up to a church called The Church of Open Door. As we walked through the main doors and into the sanctuary, I thought of the words my father said years before: "I will never step foot in church again."

During worship, Dad sat in his seat wearing his sunglasses like he normally did, but the presence of God was so powerful that he began weeping uncontrollably. It was as if Jesus had been trying to tell my dad all along, "Chuck, I am right here." The pastor got up and said, "Ya know what? We were supposed to start a new sermon series today, but I feel like God told me not to start that today but to preach one more time on immorality." Every word the pastor preached that day was handpicked by God for my dad's heart to hear. It was such a surreal moment watching my dad step foot in church again, but seeing him encounter Jesus was even more beautiful.

A few months later, our family received devastating news that my cousin, who wasn't much older than me, had taken his life. His tragic death shook our family. During the drive to the funeral, my dad said, "Son, they have asked me to share a message at the funeral today. I am going to start the message, but then I want you to close and give the altar call." My dream of one day preaching with my dad was becoming a reality in the least expected way. On our drive home that night, my dad told me he wanted to preach with me more. He talked about ministry we could do together and one day having tent revivals. My eyes got big and my heart became full as I was seeing a shift in my dad's heart.

Then May 3rd came.

I was playing softball on a gorgeous summer night. The sun was setting, and life was going well until I heard someone yelling my name from the dugout and that I needed to leave the game. My sister was watching the game that night, and she'd received a phone call that Dad had been in another motorcycle accident. Now, I know what you are all thinking: "Your dad was still riding motorcycles even with an amputated leg?" Yes. Yes, he was. My dad didn't see limitation. He never viewed life on those terms. He'd had a passion for motorcycles for as long as I could remember. As we were on our way to the hospital, I remember feeling calm and that everything would be fine. After all, my dad had been in several motorcycle accidents in my lifetime.

When we arrived, the doctor told us that my dad was breathing, and we would be able to visit with him in a little while. We were in the waiting room for two hours, but it felt more like ten. I went to find someone to see what was going on, and a doctor asked if we could all talk somewhere else. Once we were in the room, he shut the door and told us some of the findings, but it seemed as if he was kind of beating around the bush. Someone spoke up and said, "Doctor, just tell it to us straight. What is happening with Chuck?" The doctor looked at us and gave us the news we all feared. He said, "We found out that his brain stem was completely crushed and has no activity. His heart is beating, and we have him hooked up. You guys can let me know what you decide to do. I am sorry to give you this news." Everyone began to cry. I couldn't handle it. It was as if someone punched me square in the gut, knocking the wind out of me, and I collapsed into the arms of two of my friends. A few moments later, the doctor cleared my dad's room so we could say our goodbyes. I never imagined that saying goodbye to my father would be so tragic and sudden. It wasn't supposed to work this way. This wasn't the plan. My dad was supposed to meet my wife and attend our wedding. He was supposed to meet my kids and be a grandpa.

I left the hospital early to get away from everyone. When I got home, I went straight downstairs into my bedroom and collapsed onto the bed, screaming and crying as loud as I could. I felt a pain so deep that words could not describe. As I was pouring out my heart in anguish, something happened that I will never forget. It was as if Jesus Himself entered my bedroom and held me in His arms as He cried, too. I felt an embrace that couldn't have been from anyone else, and His peace flooded my mind and heart. Jesus wept when His good friend Lazarus died. Jesus wept with those who were crying and mourning, too. Surely, Jesus was trying to communicate something to Mary and Martha that day. "I AM RIGHT HERE. I am right here. I will sit with you and cry. I will sit with you and comfort you." I had never felt so close to God before that moment.

In the middle of my greatest loss and sadness, I was being held and comforted by Jesus Himself. I now knew what fatherlessness felt like. I knew the pain of not having a dad to call and ask hard questions about life. I no longer had a dad who could put his arm around me and tell me that everything was going to be okay. But I understood the character and nature of God in a different way. I understood and experienced His promise to me that He would be a Father to the fatherless, that all along He was telling me, "Micah, I am right here. I am in your present. You never have to walk through life alone." The Bible describes Jesus as "The Good Shepherd." We are the sheep. A good shepherd knows his flock and the flock knows the voice of the good shepherd. When a sheep is injured, a good shepherd carries it and does what he has to do to help the sheep heal. Psalm 68:19 says that God carries us in His arms every day. What I needed in my grief was for God to carry me, because I couldn't carry myself. A good shepherd lets his sheep know, "I am right here."

Martha and Mary learned a valuable lesson. Not only did Jesus get the final word about the past, He cared to live in their present. Jesus says that He won't leave us as orphans. He says that He will be with us every day of our lives, that He will never leave us or forsake us. I cannot tell you how many nights I have cried myself to sleep in anguish only to discover that all along He was catching every tear. I have seen Him walk with me and care for me in powerful ways. I have watched Him provide for me like a good father provides for his family. I have witnessed His blessings where there were supposed to be curses.

I want to speak into your life and encourage you with this: On your worst days, He is saying, "I AM RIGHT HERE." The God in the Bible is the same God who came to be "God with us."

Little did I know that the first and only time I would ever preach with my dad would be a couple of months before he passed away. I had experienced the greatest loss in my life, but I was just beginning to realize how near Jesus actually is and that HE holds the future.

Chapter 5

An Unknown Future

Have you ever learned terrible news and been filled with worry and anxiety about your future? I find that it happens to me more often than not.

Currently, something is happening around the world that will be told in history books for years to come. We are living through a pandemic caused by a deadly disease called COVID-19. This virus is killing thousands as I write this. In times like these, a common thought among many is, "How does this impact my future?"

When I first found out about the virus and what it can do, fear set in and anxiety within me skyrocketed when I realized that my entire future will look differently. I was listening to news reports, and one that really shook me was Imperial College's prediction of the damage the virus could do and that it could impact us for around a year and half. I immediately began to press play on the movie in my mind concerning what would happen to my wife and kids. I thought about how it would affect our ministry and home. I went into survival mode and started planning how we could ration food and how long we could go without having to visit the grocery store. I tried to find budget cuts within my salary and ministry to see how long we could survive financially. I had thoughts of losing our house and not being able to make mortgage payments.

When major life events happen. we can begin spiraling out of control when we set our minds on the future. We can begin to feel overwhelmed by the impact the event could have on our families and immediate world. I wonder if this is why Jesus said, "Don't worry about tomorrow and what tomorrow will bring."

Martha and Mary must have been in a similar spot when they lost their brother, knowing their future was suddenly altered and life would look differently forever. When you lose a loved one, certain triggers come into play and begin to affect your future. Holidays are one of mine. When the family comes together and your dad isn't there anymore, it triggers feelings of grief. Other triggers are birthdays and music. It's not uncommon for me to hear a certain song by Coldplay or U2 and get emotional thinking of my dad.

I'm sure Mary and Martha had fond memories of
Lazarus that would forever be engrained in their minds.
Maybe it was the way Lazarus laughed, or the way he lit
up when he talked about a passion of his. Maybe it was
the quirky things about Lazarus that they would always
remember. Regardless, there was only one person who
could impact the future more than the death of their
brother was going to. Jesus holds the whole world in His
hands, and He happened to be their friend.

Jesus is omniscient. He was the only one who could
understand what the future held. Even when He told
Martha, "Your brother will rise again," she didn't think
He meant right then. She thought Jesus was referring to
in the last days. Martha wasn't imagining a shift would
happen then and there, but God's thoughts and ways
are higher than ours.

Jesus knew that His listeners battled everyday fears of
the future just like you and me. He understands human
emotions and hearts better than anyone else. Jesus
knew the pressures that the everyday Jewish family

experienced. He knew they hoped to see the world power called Rome be overthrown so they could have some normalcy in their lives. Jesus understood the persecution the Jews would endure in those days and the days to come. In Matthew 6:25-34, during part of His famous Sermon on the Mount, He told them how to respond:

"Therefore I tell you, do not worry about your life, what you will eat or drink; or about your body, what you will wear. Is not life more than food, and the body more than clothes? Look at the birds of the air; they do not sow or reap or store away in barns, and yet your heavenly Father feeds them. Are you not much more valuable than they? Can any one of you by worrying add a single hour to your life? And why do you worry about clothes? See how the flowers of the field grow. They do not labor or spin. Yet I tell you that not even Solomon in all his splendor was dressed like one of these. If that is how God clothes the grass of the field, which is here today and tomorrow is thrown into the fire, will he not much more clothe you—you of little faith? So do not worry, saying, 'What shall we eat?' or 'What shall we drink?' or 'What shall we wear?' For the pagans run after all these things, and your heavenly Father knows that you need them. But seek first his kingdom and his righteousness, and all these things will be given to you as well. Therefore do not worry about tomorrow, for tomorrow will worry about itself. Each day has enough trouble of its own."

No matter who you are, it's difficult to pursue Jesus and not worry about the future when your life is falling apart. Jesus rises above all of it and challenges our faith in the middle of hardship. He asks us not to worry and to instead put things into perspective, seeking first His kingdom.

Martha and Mary were in for a treat the day Jesus showed up. Whenever He walked into a room, things shifted. When He arrived, He couldn't help but reflect the nature and character of His heavenly Father. Jesus prayed that God's kingdom would come on Earth just as it is in heaven. Wherever Jesus walked, He brought the realities of heaven along with Him. That was the reason so many were drawn to Him. He was fully man and fully God, and people experienced heaven when He was around. All Jesus had to do was speak or touch a person and they would be healed. His compassion was on full display within every miracle, including when He came to Lazarus' tomb.

If you want to know what God is like, just look at and study Jesus. Every time Jesus was moved with compassion, He always followed it with action. I want to stop really quickly and challenge you with something. Whenever you are moved deeply with compassion, don't let it be just an emotion. Always allow it to encourage you to act.

John 11:38 says, "Jesus, once more deeply moved, came to the tomb. It was a cave with a stone laid across the entrance." This was one of the most powerful moments in Jesus' ministry. He probably had tears streaming down His face, but Jesus had saved His best miracle for last and death was about to meet its master. Jesus was about to perform the final public miracle of His life and ministry during the peak time of travel for Jewish families. The Passover festival was just around the corner, and thousands of families would be traveling from outside the city into Jerusalem. The tombs were on the outside of the city, which meant all of the travelers would be walking by and stopping to watch what would happen when this rabbi named Jesus spoke to a tomb.

Jesus wept with Mary and comforted her, but their weeping was about to be replaced with laughter and joy. Psalm 30:5 tells us that "weeping only lasts for a night, but joy always comes in the morning." Jesus has a way of exchanging our tears and pain for joy and a smile!

In John 11:39, Jesus says, "Take away the stone." It was not customary to roll away a tombstone after someone was laid to rest. The body would have already begun decomposing, and there would have been a terrible odor. Martha spoke up, "But Lord, by this time there is a bad odor, for he has been there four days." She clearly didn't understand what was about to take place. The response Jesus gave her is classic. Jesus says in reply, "Did I not tell you that if you believe, you will see the glory of God?"

I'm convinced that following Jesus is about endurance more than it is about moments. In Matthew 24, Jesus says, "Those who endure to the end will be saved." Life will throw you all sorts of curveballs, but those who hold onto Jesus and keep the faith will watch some of the most extraordinary events play out.

I have come to look at problems as opportunities for God to demonstrate His goodness. Whenever something horrible happens in my life, I look for the moment when God will be glorified. He loves to work things out for the good of those who love Him and are called according to His purposes. He loves to work through us and bring His glory to the earth.

If I could pass on one piece of advice to anyone reading this book, it would be to hold onto Jesus for the long haul and don't ever let go. Whatever you do, don't stop believing. You will experience times of doubt, fear and questioning; however, take your doubt, fear and unbelief to the feet of Jesus and say, "Jesus, would you help me with my unbelief?" You might be on the verge of breakthrough. You might just be on the brink of a miracle! I want to challenge and encourage you to keep holding on. Don't give up. Your life is so precious to Jesus that He says you are more valuable than the birds of the air and the lilies of the field. If the birds of the air and the lilies of the field don't need to worry, than neither do you and I. God has a plan for your life and even though there are times it feels like hell, He is ready to take the worst things and turn them into something beautiful.

The worry that enters your mind day and night will never add a moment or bring value to your life. So, exchange it for prayer and let God be God. When was the last time you experienced His peace in the middle of your worry? True peace is not an absence of problems or worry. Peace is knowing that, even though wicked storms surround you, you are loved and valued by a mighty, strong and all-powerful God.

If you saw your child in the middle of a busy street, what would you do? You would do what every parent would do—RUN, pick him up and bring him to safety. How much more does your heavenly Father want to RUN and uphold you? He is so good that He will get down and cry with you. He is so good that He will comfort you and bring peace in the middle of what feels like chaos. Not only will He bring peace, but He wants to demonstrate His power in your life. There is a wonderful story waiting to be written through your life. **Even though the future is unknown to you, there is one who knows and holds your future—Jesus.**

When Jesus showed up that day in Bethany, He encountered two sisters weeping, afraid of the future and mourning their loss. When He came to the tomb and said, "Take away the stone," things were merely getting started. Journey with me to see the breakthrough and miracles that happen when you hold onto Jesus long enough to watch Him do what He does best. Death to life.

Chapter 6

Death to Life

Whenever someone experiences a miracle, it's always for the glory of Jesus, the one who provided the miracle. The person who experiences the miracle has an opportunity to go and share what Jesus did for them.

When I refer to the word "death", I am referring to any and all kinds of sin, lostness, hurt, pain, destruction, theft, evil, and even death itself. When you study Jesus' life and watch how His ministry unfolded, He was constantly encountering dead things and bringing them back to life. After all, Jesus came to bring heaven to Earth. Everything in the earth is passing away and has an expiration date, but heaven is eternal.

The story of Jesus encountering a man whom society feared and isolated from always fascinates me. You could very well say this was a "dead man walking." In Mark 5, Jesus rolled up to the Gentile side of the Sea of Galilee. You would rarely find Jewish people walking into

Gentile territory, as their beliefs did not mix. I love how Jesus intentionally led His disciples into a scandalous area. Everything He does is done with purpose. Jesus was purposefully demonstrating what it meant to follow Him, which included going places others didn't want to go. Being His disciple meant reaching people who were broken, lost and hurting.

It just so happens that Jesus led His disciples to the very person He wanted them to encounter. When they arrived on shore, the disciples came face-to-face with a naked, screaming, demoniac man who had cuts, scars and bloody, open wounds all over himself. I don't know about you, but the minute I see a dude like that, I am straight up bouncing. Not Jesus, though. He had a plan to see a man go from death to life. The Bible describes this man as someone who screamed day and night, and he lived among the tombs. Essentially, he lived among dead people. He felt more comfortable living among the dead than he did among the living. Everything about this guy signaled "weirdo, pervert, psycho, demon possessed." People had tried to bind him up with chains, but he always broke through them. The Bible mentions that no one was strong enough to subdue him. But he had yet to encounter Christ.

Jesus led His disciples by boat through an intense storm, and they'd watched as He rebuked the storm and calmed the lake. They were about to watch a demon possessed man freed by the power of Jesus, who saw what every other human missed about the man. Jesus didn't see a perverted, weirdo, psycho, naked, self-harming man. He saw someone made in His image who He couldn't wait to set free. We often see ourselves through our scars, but Jesus sees a different version of us. He sees who we can become when we're set free in Him. Jesus came to take the dead things in our lives and see them resurrected to life. The man went from screaming his head off and charging Jesus and His disciples to sitting peacefully and fully clothed at the feet of Jesus. Jesus took authority over the legion of demons that lived in the man, and the demons begged Jesus to be driven into a herd of pigs. When they occupied the pigs, the pigs ran off the cliff and into the Sea of Galilee.

Whatever dead things are in you were crucified when Jesus Himself was crucified on the cross. The dead things no longer get to define you. You get to receive the free gift of Jesus' love and salvation. That day a man who couldn't be controlled or tied down with chains was liberated from the grip of death and demonic possession. He was given over to the resurrection life and power that come through our Savior, Jesus Christ.

I love what happens next, though. The man who was radically changed wanted to follow Jesus. I don't blame him. If I were set free like that, I would want to go wherever Jesus went, too. Nonetheless, Jesus commissioned the man. He told him to go back to his town and tell everyone what happened to him. In other words, go and share! Go and tell everyone about how you were set free. Show them the scars as evidence that I healed your once opened wounds.

The man's testimony carried weight, because the demons had left, and the presence of Jesus had taken over him. We know he did what Jesus told him, because the next time Jesus visited the Decapolis, there were large groups of people waiting to meet the Messiah. People were lining up to be healed.

Within 24 hours, the disciples had seen a storm obey Jesus' voice and a possessed man freed because of His authority over evil spirits. If you continue to follow along in Mark 5, you'll read about them going back to the other side of the lake and meeting a desperate father whose daughter was dying. By the time Jesus arrived, the little girl was dead. But when He walked into her room, everything changed. Jesus raised her from the dead! The disciples were given a front row seat and commissioned to go and do likewise: to preach the gospel, heal those who needed healing, and deliver those who had demonic spirits. Jesus was establishing His new kingdom through ordinary people like you and me who will tell of God's goodness and how He loves to lead people into His everlasting life.

Lazarus had been dead for four days. What Jesus had done so often was about to happen again. Someone who was dead was about to take his first breath since being locked in a grave. After Jesus told the people to remove the tombstone, He said a prayer to His heavenly Father. He gave thanks to God for the miracle that was about to take place. He prayed that, for the sake of those present, MANY would believe in Jesus as Messiah and, ultimately, give glory to God. Even up until His final miracle, Jesus was giving His Father thanks and honor.

With a loud voice, Jesus yelled out and said, "Lazarus, COME OUT!" I love how Scripture says Jesus called out in a loud voice, because I can imagine myself standing there next to Him, watching God Himself shouting over a dead body from a distance and seeing the drama unfold.

The same breath that spoke all of creation into existence, that created man, is the same breath used to speak over dead things and see them come to life. God's voice and breath have the authority to create, heal, set free, and resurrect. This is why I wrote this book. I can't resist sharing how God resurrected dead things in my own life. I wouldn't be here today if it weren't for the breath and voice of God reaching a young, hurting man—*me*.

Growing up in a broken home, I remember Mom sharing her fears of not being able to pay the mortgage because she wasn't sure if my dad was going to pay child support. I watched her consider different options of what we'd do if we were going to lose the house. My mother consulted with me about decisions for the future. The weight of my own future was upon my shoulders, and it felt more like a heavy chain wrapped around my neck. I recall feeling so lost about college and what I should do with my life. I never really asked my parents for money, because I was afraid of how they would react and knew the answer would likely be "no."

What really troubled me was watching my eight-year-old sister fight for her life. It felt as though my family's second home was the children's hospital. We were always there visiting her and encouraging her along, but I felt caught between my parents when it came to my sister. We visited fundraisers for other kids who also had cancer, and I heard about funerals for kids we'd met in the hospital who didn't make it. Death was always a potential reality for my sister. Sitting and thinking about the future and losing my youngest sister to cancer was troubling. I remember when we discovered that the tumors had spread to her lungs. Typically, when cancer spreads to the lungs, it only gets worse. To try to get rid of the tumors, she had over fifteen surgeries and battled all the chemotherapy and radiation her little body could handle.

One day, the Make a Wish foundation showed up and offered my sister a wish. It's an amazing foundation that grants children a wish when they and their families are facing hardship. Victoria's wish was to swim with the dolphins in Florida and go to Walt Disney World. The trip was supposed to be a magical getaway for a young girl fighting for her life, but any sort of happiness was constantly snuffed out by our parents' arguments. Those days were extremely difficult. However, there was someone in the middle of cancer who held my sister's future, and I was called not to worry but to seek first His kingdom. There were thousands of people praying for God to miraculously heal my sister. With the prognosis and her having a twenty percent chance of survival, we needed a divine healing.

An evangelist who had heard about my sister fighting for her life visited our church one day. I remember him prophesying that God would heal Victoria of cancer and that she would go to his church in Tennessee to share the testimony of how God healed her. He took my sister and our family into a back room to pray over her once more. He prayed that the fire of God would come down and burn up the cancer in her body. We had been praying for over two years that we'd see a breakthrough. Well, little did we know that the miracle worker, Jesus, was going to show up that night. When my sister went to the hospital to get the usual scans to check where tumors were in her body, the doctors couldn't find any. Through the power of medicine and a healing touch from Jesus, there was NO MORE CANCER IN HER BODY!

Jesus decided to show up in His great timing and heal my sister that day. She has been cancer free now for over fifteen years, and the doctors at the hospital called her "The Miracle Child." God has a way of writing stories that continually consist of moving people from death to life, and I witnessed Him do that very thing with my sister.

Growing up in our house was difficult, because I remembered what life was like before the divorce. It was filled with so much joy, fun and happiness. But moments leading up to, during and after the divorce, made home a tough place to find peace and rest. When you experience trauma or hard times, it can be tough to want to go back to the spaces where you experienced them. We often run away and want nothing to do with the places of pain and destruction in our lives.

The house I grew up in is the house where I saw my dad bring hard drugs and try to hide them from me. The house I grew up in is the house where I heard my dad stumble around drunk when he came home late from the bar. The house I grew up in is the house where Mom and Dad had loud fights, where I recall my dad being arrested because of an altercation with my mom. The house I grew up in was filled with the pain of my siblings and me sitting in our living room and hearing that our parents were getting a divorce. The house I grew up in is where we lived when my sister received a cancer diagnosis and was given a twenty percent chance to live. The house I grew up in, where I saw immorality and impurity run rampant, is the VERY HOUSE THAT MY WIFE AND I PURCHASED on October 6, 2016.

I CAN'T MAKE THIS STUFF UP. When I was at the title company with my mom, the realtor and title workers, my mom looked at me and said, "Micah, do you know what today is?" I replied, "No, Mom. I have no clue." She said, "Today is your dad and my wedding anniversary." My jaw dropped, and I began to smile. My parents were married on October 6, 1984.

God has a sense of humor. The first home my parents ever purchased was the first home my wife and I purchased. The very rooms that once told a story of darkness and death are now rooms that remind me of the grace, power, and love of Jesus. I now get to raise my own family in this house, and I don't think about the evil that took place here. Instead, I think about the power of a great God who took dead things and is turning them around for life and peace in Him. Every day I watch as my own children grow up in this house. They don't know the story yet, but one day I will get to tell them about the faithfulness of God and how He redeems and restores broken things. God has a way of writing your story way better than you ever could.

Just like a demoniac man was set free and had a story to tell, I now get to tell my story all over America and bring hope to thousands of teenagers every year. I get to point to Jesus as the one who can take your story and turn it into a masterpiece.

Countless people believed in Jesus on the day He resurrected Lazarus. In fact, many couldn't wait to see Lazarus themselves, because the story got around and blew up all over Jerusalem. The stories God writes are intended to bring hope and life to all those who might hear them.

Your story isn't finished yet. Remember when Jesus told Martha to believe and that, if she would trust Him, she would see God get all the glory? I want to encourage you. Wherever you are today, your story isn't done. Jesus gets the final word on your past. He's a Savior who loves to live in your present, and you'd better believe HE HOLDS YOUR FUTURE. Jesus always gets the credit and the glory when you surrender the pen of your life back into His hands.

The sad reality is that so many of us never taste true freedom or experience a resurrection from the grave we find ourselves in. We keep going back to the same things over and over, and the reality of a grave seems more real than the reality of being resurrected. Sometime after Lazarus was raised from the dead, someone else was resurrected: Jesus Himself. He didn't stay in a grave, and you don't have to either. The grave couldn't hold Jesus, and it won't hold you.

PART 2

LIFE ABOVE THE GRAVE

Proverbs 15:24 in the New Living Translation says, "The path of the wise leads to life above; they leave the grave behind."

Lazarus woke up from his four-day death and left that grave behind. Just how Christ raised him up to walk away from his grave, He does the same thing for you and me. Our graves can be a range of different things. Your grave might be a gambling addiction, rough marriage, bad family life, or any of the variety of things that try to bring us down.

Jesus emphasized a life away from the grave and eternity with Him. The God we worship can't be found in a grave but happens to be sitting right next to His heavenly Father.

I want to break down the "how to" in living a life above

the grave. I am now 34 years old. I'm still learning what it means to leave the grave behind, but what I have come to experience and live out is essential for any person choosing to go from death to life.

Jesus made it possible to leave the grave behind. In the coming chapters, you will see that you, too, can leave your grave behind.

Part two BEGINS NOW.

Chapter 7

The New You

I woke up to my wife hovering over the top of me, saying, "Micah, I think today is the day." I'd been to some birthing classes and remembered the stages of labor. I thought I had some time from what I remembered, so I rolled back over into my bed to get more sleep. I could hear my wife moaning and groaning in the bathroom, and it's hard to get more sleep when you hear your wife in labor.

I'd borrowed the church van and left my car at church the night before. I looked at Steph and said, "Hey, babe, I will be right back. I am going to go take the van back to church and get my car." After I parked the van, I went inside the building to speak to some of the staff. I took my time chatting, saying, "Hey, you guys, today could be the day!" I thought I had all the time in the world. But by the time I got home, the moans were louder, and my wife was visibly in pain. Something inside told me I needed to get my wife to the hospital NOW. When we arrived, the nurse said, "Oh, wow, this baby is coming now. You're at a nine." If you are like me and didn't know what nine means, it means the baby is coming out!

August 19, 2016 is a day that forever changed me. After Steph held Everleigh Dawn, the nurse handed her to me. I'd envisioned what it would be like to hold my firstborn. I wanted my first words over my daughter's life to be a prayer. Right there in the hospital room, with nurses all around, I began to cry and pray for her. I prayed and prophesied over her life. As I held my little girl, I had a revelation of my own.

The last time I had been in that hospital was the day my dad died from his motorcycle accident, and now I was holding a brand-new life. I was watching God perform a miracle right before my eyes. Where death was once a reality, life was being birthed right in front of me. The grave had once been before me at this hospital, but I was seeing life come from the grave. Everleigh had arrived and life above the grave was real.

The gospel is a lot like that. Even though death and sin may be our current reality, Scripture talks about a new birth we get to experience. 2 Corinthians 5:17 tells us that when we receive the truth that Jesus took the death we deserved upon Himself and begin to follow Him, the "old self" is gone and a new creation is born. I will never get tired of watching people transform right in front of me. I have heard about and encountered numerous people who were once far from Christ and now speak about the transformation that took place when Jesus entered their story.

Jesus' life and ministry constantly pointed to life above the grave. Everywhere Jesus went, He brought with Him the resurrecting power that would touch broken bodies and make them whole. He would encounter chief tax collectors, then watch them give their money away to the poor. His love transformed individuals and impacted the multitudes.

The first step toward living life above the grave and operating in your God-given freedom is to believe and walk forth in the gospel every day. My youth pastor once gave us a unique challenge to apply a practice he also tried to implement regularly: spending every morning in prayer and speaking the gospel over himself. He'd roll out of bed, get down on his knees, then thank

God for saving him and showing him mercy and grace. I think this is extremely significant, because we'll start our day reminded of God's great grace and favor toward us.

Ephesians 2:1-5 says it like this: "As for you, you were dead in your transgressions and sins in which you used to live when you followed the ways of this world and of the ruler of the kingdom of the air, the spirit who is now at work in those who are disobedient. All of us also lived among them at one time, gratifying the cravings of our flesh and following its desires and thoughts. Like the rest, we were by nature deserving of wrath. But because of his great love for us, God, who is rich in mercy, made us alive with Christ even when we were dead in transgressions—it is by grace you have been saved."

This is what it's all about. This is what my youth pastor was trying to tell us. Every day, he reminds himself that he was a dead man—dead in his sins, dead in his transgressions—and what he deserved was the wrath of God. Verse four hits us with the BIG BUT: "But because of his great love for us, God, who is rich in mercy, made us alive with Christ even when we were dead in transgressions—it is by grace you have been saved." That's really good news! That's the way to live life above the grave, the starting point of a fully alive life. This scripture clearly shows us how God brings us into life everlasting as well as how little it has to do with us and focuses instead on the greatness of God. Other religions will have you working your way to earn God's salvation, but Ephesians describes His salvation as a free gift offered through grace.

When I look back on my own life, I am still humbled that Jesus didn't just save me once, but I am being saved and made new every day. The gospel is the Good News for you and me. Sometimes it sounds too good to be true, but it was the only way there could ever be restored relationship between humanity and God. As a follower of Christ, His grace is what sustains you and empowers you to live life above the grave. Without it, loving God would be impossible. Grace doesn't just overlook offense; it empowers you to live a life fully above the grave.

The apostle Paul was passionate about seeing followers of Jesus grasp this concept of freedom in Christ. He spends a good portion of time in the book of Romans talking about the truth and reality of what Jesus accomplished for us. Romans 6 says that you and I are no longer slaves to sin, but because Christ died for us, we have died to sin. When Christ was crucified on the cross, our sin was crucified along with Him. When Jesus took the cross, our sinful nature also died. Because Jesus resurrected, because He lives, we can come alive in Him. We are resurrected with His power to live a NEW LIFE above the grave. The dead weight of sin is no longer our master. According to Scripture, the old self, the old life, is dead to sin.

Because of God's love, we get to start each day from a place of renewal. God's word says that His mercies are new every morning, so we never have to earn His affection or His forgiveness. Both are freely offered as gifts, and all we have to do is receive them. The work Christ can do within us is beautifully extraordinary, but we will never walk in newness if we don't receive the truth of what He did for us. Freedom can come instantly, but continual freedom is a process of everlasting grace and empowerment. I have been a follower of Christ for over 27 years. In those years, I have battled all sorts of temptation and trials. The longer I've followed Him, the more internal freedom I've experienced, and the thought of sin has grown more and more undesirable.

A key moment in my freedom took place at an altar in Alexandria, Minnesota, during a youth retreat at a campground called Lake Geneva Christian Center. I was there to preach during the morning sessions, but the night speaker was an evangelist by the name of Eric Samuel Timm. As the message was ending that Wednesday night, students were coming up front for prayer believing for breakthrough and freedom. I heard Eric say, "Where is Micah? Is Micah in the building?" I remember thinking, "Why in the world does he want me to come down to the front?" As I walked to meet him at the front of the stage, he began to speak prophetically over my life. He said, "Micah, you have been preaching from pain and fear. Tonight, that pain and fear stop here. Micah, I want you to speak out loud every fear that you have carried and held onto in your life, because tonight God is going to heal and deliver you. Micah, your story is going to be like a rod and staff that tap on hard rocks, hard hearts, so that water might gush forth again. Micah, God is going to use your story to help bring freedom to so many others." He then had two of my friends lift my arms in the air just as Aaron and Hur had done for Moses. My friends began to pray freedom over my life as I wept and began to leave fear at the altar.

Before that night, I was afraid of marriage. I had dated

Steph, who was my girlfriend at the time, for about two years, and the thought of marriage scared me. I saw the pain my mother endured with my father, and I never wanted to hurt a woman like that. I was afraid that one day I might inflict the same pain on my own wife. So, whenever I thought about marriage, I tried to shove it out of my mind. But God had freedom in store for me that night. Eric was sensitive to the Holy Spirit and bold enough to speak freedom into my life in front of over 600 students. While my friends were praying on either side of me, I began to list every fear and pain I'd been holding onto. As I was confessing to God, I felt some sort of liquid being dumped all over me. I had no idea what it was, but I started to feel free for the first time. I found out after the fact that Eric dumped five bottles of anointing oil on me. I had been doused in oil, but even more than that, Jesus Himself was delivering me and setting me free to live life above the grave. That was a defining moment in my life. Two months later, I proposed to my girlfriend and we were married five months after that. I preached differently. I spoke differently. Fear and sin were no longer my master. Christ's freedom reached me, a hurting and broken young man, and allowed me to walk above the pain of the past. Jesus set me free with just one touch.

I want you to know that freedom is freely given, and I want you to make a list of every fear and heartache that is holding you back. Write them down, then take that list to a pastor or friend who can pray boldly over your life to experience the freedom and grace of Christ. Afterward, I want you to rip up the list and throw it away, because those things don't belong to you anymore.

Fear can keep you from the path God has for you. Only Jesus can make a way for you to continually be free. His grace saved you and His grace is the only thing that can sustain you. You are a new creation, made for good works. Don't let the grave get the final word. Allow what Jesus did to lead you to life above the grave. When you follow Him, fear gets to die so that life can come.

Your process of freedom is just getting started. God's power and grace led Lazarus out of the grave, but the people around him helped him take off his grave clothes and stay free. Keep going with me as we continue our journey from death to life.

Chapter 8

No One Alone

"God sets the lonely in families." — Psalm 68:6

When I was recently interviewed for a podcast, the host said to me, "Micah, it sounds like you have experienced a lot of trauma in your life. How would you instruct someone on how to make it through like you did and come out better on the other side?" He put me on the spot. I had never been asked that question before, and he didn't prep me before the interview. But a couple of thoughts immediately came to mind.

The best decision a single mom ever made was picking up the phone to call her friend and ask, "Where is the best church I can bring my family to?" The next Sunday, my family and I showed up at Cedar Valley Church in Bloomington, Minnesota. I was around 13 years old, and I was the last person who wanted to go to church. Our previous church had split, and I missed the people and relationships I had there.

We pulled into the parking lot and Mom said, "Okay, kids, let's get out and go inside," but I told her I was staying put. The thought of going into a large church where I didn't know anybody was frightening and added to the mixed emotions I was already experiencing because of our unstable home. I told Mom there was nothing she could do to get me into church that day. Growing impatient, she looked at me and said, "If you don't get out of the van and come into church, I am going to go find a man and bring him outside to drag your butt inside." I just knew there was no way she would actually do that. Surely enough, minutes later, I saw some random man walking outside the church with my mom. I immediately hid under the backseat, thinking my mom wouldn't see me, but moms are clever. They know how their own kids think. The next thing I knew, the van door opened, and the man was staring at me underneath the seat. He said, "Son, you need to obey your mom and get out of the van and come inside." Reluctantly, I got out with my head down, dragging and fuming mad that my mom would embarrass me that way.

Little did I know that God would use this local church to bring about some of the greatest personal freedom of my entire life. He began healing my heart during a tumultuous time. Within a couple of Sundays, I met Chris Rausch, who became my best friend and the best man in my wedding years later. God knew that I would never experience His freedom and life above the grave apart from His church and His family. John 11:44 is a scripture that can sometimes be overlooked when talking about Lazarus' resurrection. It reads, "The dead man came out, his hands and feet wrapped with strips of linen, and a cloth around his face. Jesus said to them, 'Take off the grave clothes and let him go.'"

I think it's powerful that Jesus demonstrated a miracle. However, in order for Lazarus to fully walk away from the grave and live free, he was going to need others to help him get out of his grave clothes. Jesus knew that, within a few days, He was going to die on a cross and be resurrected. He also knew that on Pentecost fifty days later, something called the "church" was going to be birthed and launched around the world. It would set people free from the power of sin and help them stay free.

The church was God's idea. The Greek word for "church" is *ekklesia*, and it doesn't refer to a building or four walls. It describes a gathering or assembly of people. The plan God had all along was to build a family. In Acts 2, we read about people gathering as they waited for the gift of the Holy Spirit to show up. When the Holy Spirit fell that day, 3,000 people became believers in Jesus Christ and began preaching the gospel. The local church had started.

It's possible to believe in Jesus but never ditch the grave clothes. How many of us still walk around wearing them even though we believe, know and love Jesus? This is exactly why we need Godly community, to help us take off the grave clothes and become the men and women God is calling us to become. Isolation was never God's design. If God wanted that, He would have just created man and never created woman. He saw that it wasn't good for man to be alone, so He created a companion for man to do life with. God didn't need to make humans in His image, but He did and it was His pleasure to make mankind to be in relationship with one another. God delights in placing the lonely in families.

However, when we read the creation story, we see the consequences of mankind's disobedience to God and choosing sin for the very first time. Innocence was exchanged with guilt. Purity was exchanged with shame, and grave clothes were worn for the first time. Adam and Eve realized they were naked and felt ashamed, so they made clothes to hide their bodies. I find it interesting that they made clothes to cover their shame. They began to take matters into their own hands, which was the first sign of being disconnected from God. Because of His grace, God pursued them in the middle of their disobedience. In Genesis 3, He called out, "Where are you?" and shared a prophetic word about a new plan that would come to pass, one that would restore right relationship between God and man. It required the death of His Son, Jesus, so that we might be set free from the power of sin and learn to live above the grave.

Man's decision to forsake the truth of God's Word for a lie has damaging effects. Many people in the church today are still caught up in addictions and feel as though it is a normal way of life or how it always has to be. Plenty of "Christians" are struggling in their marriages. Teenagers are battling issues and bad habits. But the same God who pursued Adam and Eve in their sin is the same God who pursues us. He desires for all of us to be free and walk away from our grave clothes.

Not long ago I was at an Apple store to get something repaired. While I was at the counter waiting for an employee, a customer next to me was being helped regarding an issue with the charging port on her laptop. The employee went to the back room and brought out a small tool, and within five seconds he removed a small object that had been stuck in the port. He looked at the customer and said, "Okay, all fixed now." The young lady looked back at the employee and said, "Really? That's all it was? I thought it would be this way forever." The employee laughed and assured her that the port was back to functioning at one hundred percent.

Just like this young lady thought she'd have issues with her laptop forever, many of us live our lives never tasting the freedom that Christ has always made available to us. Christ is like the employee who sees our deepest wounds and the healing we need. He goes and gets a "tool" called the local church, using it to help bring freedom to millions who follow Him. To God, our problems are like small pebbles stuck in a charging port. When we think our habits and sinful patterns are impossible to break, God sees them through His Son's blood on the cross, which washes us clean and gives us hope, freedom, and a brand-new start in Him. In Jesus' hands, we can live renewed and pure lives because of

His righteousness. Whom the Son sets free is free indeed.

Jesus could have done ministry by Himself, but He chose twelve people to bring into His inner circle and call His disciples. He chose to do things in community. God made us for Himself and for each other. Jesus boils the two greatest commandments down to loving Him and loving people. Therefore, true and lasting freedom is found in the confines of His plan, which is Godly community. His church was meant to be on mission in making disciples and baptizing them in the name of the Father, Son, and Holy Spirit.

In the Great Commission, Jesus instructed the disciples to go and make more disciples. Another way to say it is, "Go and EXTEND THE FAMILY. Go and invite others into the family. Go and find the fatherless. Go and find the widows. Go and find the poor. Go and find the hurting and the defenseless. Go and find the lonely, because I have a place for them in my family."

As a young man, I didn't know I needed a bigger family. I had no idea that God's plan of freedom in my life would be to place me in the context of a larger family that would take me in, cry with me, defend me, and pray with me. I didn't know that God would use hundreds of people over my lifetime to help me take off my grave clothes and be free. Once you find a family to grow with, it doesn't stop there. To this very day, I have a deep longing to be with the family of God to worship together, study the Bible together, and confess our sins to one another, so I can become the man God is calling me to be. When I find myself broken, I desire to be around the family of God. You would think that because I'm a minister I no longer have broken tendencies or false mindsets. However, I am human just like you and need a Godly community to grow and become like Jesus with. I am so grateful that God places the lonely in families. No one is exempt. If there is brokenness in your life, then you are officially qualified to join the family— but don't expect to stay broken. Jesus can't wait to put His restorative power to work in your life through the healing found in community.

One of the greatest tragedies today is that people believe the lie that they aren't good enough to join the local church. Too often I have listened to the stories of people who say they don't go to church because of how badly they have messed up or that they aren't good enough. If those same people could see the daily struggles that people in church face, they might see they have a place to belong, too. Many of us hide just like Adam and Eve did, but the same God who called out to find His creation is the same God calling out to the world. He made it possible for ALL to be a part of His family.

Let's be the kinds of people who match the voice and heart of Jesus, making room for others to join in and live life with us. A life above the grave is fully experienced when integrated into His family. Jesus looked at "them" and said, "Take off his grave clothes and let him go." You can stop doing life on your own now and allow others to come around you, people who will love you just as you are and into the person God is calling you to become: FREE.

Chapter 9

Forgiveness

"Father, forgive them, for they do not know what they are doing." — Luke 23:34

It was a Friday night in Jerusalem, and the city was buzzing before Sabbath started at sundown. We were scheduled to have a meal in a Jewish family's home. I distinctly remember meeting this beautiful family, and I didn't realize the life-changing effect the coming moments would have on me. There were about thirty of us American pastors in the house. The father got up to welcome each of us and described what would be happening throughout the night. We watched as they sang songs as a family. The father and his children also sang a song to the mother. It was hard not to cry seeing them honor her in their home and how simple life was through their eyes.

Before eating the meal the family prepared for us, the father asked each of us to share a highlight from our trip and something we'd learned thus far. Mostly everyone stood up to share something about how beautiful the land, people and country of Israel are. But one of my friends shared something personal that grabbed all of our attention. He said that the most impactful part of the trip was our visit to the Holocaust Museum earlier that day. He then told us that while he lived in New York City, his family had roots in Germany. He shared with us about a time when he'd come across a Nazi uniform upstairs at his grandfather's house. As he explained that his grandpa had served in the war as a Nazi soldier, he began to cry. Through his tears he said, "I want to apologize on behalf of my grandpa and family for the destruction that we caused to your family. I want to ask for forgiveness." There wasn't a dry eye in the room. My German friend then walked toward the Jewish father, reached out for a hug, and they embraced. Generations of hurt, death, and destruction were reconciled before my very eyes. Before we left that evening, the father thanked us for coming and especially thanked my friend for his compassionate actions.

Forgiveness has a way of bringing forth healing that bitterness can't. The healing that took place that night is forever etched in my mind. Without forgiveness, there is no life above the grave. All of us deserve to be dead in our sin, but in Christ's rich mercy, He loved us enough to FORGIVE US of all our sin. Whoever believes in Him will never have to experience the grave but will live above the grave with Him for eternity. One of the greatest examples of heaven on Earth is when forgiveness is offered and received. When you think about it, it is actually a lot more difficult and heroic to extend forgiveness than it is to hold onto bitterness.

One particular instance in Scripture that stands out to me is the stoning of Stephen. Stephen was a man described as being full of the Spirit and full of faith. Personally, I think that's one of the greatest compliments and descriptions of a life well lived. Stephen preached the full gospel and was hated by many because of it. Before he was killed, he echoed something similar to what Jesus said. Stephen prayed for the wrongdoers. He prayed that they would encounter God's forgiveness and be changed forever.

Forgiveness can bring about permanent change. I wonder if the prayer Stephen offered up was the key to Saul's conversion and heart transformation. Saul persecuted Christians and felt as though he was doing God a favor by trying to stop this movement called

"Christianity." He'd witnessed Stephen's death that day, but he was later called to minister to both Jews and Gentiles and wrote a significant portion of the New Testament. But before Saul ever personally encountered Christ, he experienced Him through both Stephen's life and death. Stephen was an ordinary man filled with the Holy Spirit and, while he never got to see Saul's salvation, he prayed with faith for the forgiveness of those who persecuted him. Love overcame death. Stephen lived a life above the grave. Up to his very last breath, he breathed forgiveness toward others.

One of the greatest indications of spiritual maturity is when we are able to extend forgiveness. Jesus modeled it for us first. The reason He is so passionate about forgiveness is because He understands that where there is bitterness, the enemy has room to destroy. The book of 1 John tells us that Christ came to destroy the works of the devil. Bitterness gives the devil a foothold in our lives. When Jesus takes up residence in our lives through the Holy Spirit, He prompts us to forgive so the works of the devil can be destroyed. Forgiveness is more than a physical demonstration; it requires faith and has supernatural impact.

Jesus speaks harshly and passionately about forgiveness. In Matthew 18, we read the parable of a king's servant whose debt was forgiven. Moments after he was forgiven, the same servant abused another who owed him money. Because the person was unable to pay him back, the servant had him imprisoned. When the king found out, he threw the servant into jail also. Jesus tells us that when we don't forgive others, He won't forgive us. That is one of the most loaded statements in all of Scripture, and it's the reason forgiveness isn't just a feel-good action step that we take. There are spiritual ramifications when we choose not to forgive. Forgiveness releases both the victim and the attacker and makes room for healing and reconciliation.

Stephen was the victim, and his attackers were Saul and those who stoned him. Stephen extended forgiveness even as he was being killed. That is powerful! He never got to witness the transformation in Saul's heart. However, he had faith that the forgiveness he extended left his accuser in the hands of an almighty God and not in the hands of a limited human.

Bitterness almost always does more damage than what initially wounded us. When unforgiveness isn't dealt with, it leads to death. I have witnessed firsthand the destruction bitterness causes. The pain is always worse and lasts longer when we hold onto hurt rather than offer forgiveness.

I want to make sure you know that if you've been hurt, your pain is valid and what happened to you wasn't right in any way. I also want you to know that it wasn't something God did, and He didn't want that for you. The evil we experience is not in the character and goodness of God. Pain and brokenness are the fruit of sin and the fallen world we live in. The world will tell you to hit back and fight. The world will tell you to get revenge and take life into your own hands. The world will tell you to cause even greater pain to those who hurt you, but Jesus' way—the way of life above the grave—tells us something different.

Jesus tells us to forgive those who hurt us. He tells us to pray for our enemies and to turn the other cheek. Jesus' way doesn't include revenge. The way of Jesus is forgiveness, which can take place physically, but the healing, renewal and restoration are supernatural. We do our part, and God does His part in our spirits.

I have seen bitterness destroy families, marriages, friendships ... You name it. Harboring unforgiveness not only impacts us internally but physically. When we are emotionally unhealthy, it affects the brain and our mental health as well as our physical bodies. I know people who have been healed of chronic pain, headaches, loss of sleep and more when they forgave, because they were no longer carrying weight they were never meant to carry.

I want to share seven practical steps to help you forgive others. After all, seven is God's number, or something like that ... I mean, He does tell us to forgive seventy times seven, so why not give seven practical steps?

1. Recognize how much you have been forgiven.

This will help you keep in perspective the principle Jesus mentions about the log in your own eye versus the speck in your friend's eye. Oftentimes, we forget how much God has forgiven us and how He treats us. I'm quickly humbled when reminded of my own sin and mistakes and how graciously Christ received me. When I think of how much He has forgiven me, it makes me slow to want to hurt others. Christ's perspective is far different from mine, and I recognize that I need His perspective. I'm grateful that He doesn't treat me according to what my sins deserve. And because I am a recipient of His great love and forgiveness, I now choose to operate the same way toward others.

2. Bitterness is not God's plan for your life.

In Ephesians 6, Paul talks about our spiritual battle, and he mentions that the enemy uses schemes to try to trip us up. One of those schemes is offense. The devil wants us to take offense to what others do and hold onto it, but that's not Christ's plan for our lives. When we realize that offense will only do more harm than good, we are able to see the situation objectively. It allows us to view it through the lens of Scripture and not our own emotions. If something doesn't line up with God's plan for my life, then I want nothing to do with it.

3. Press play on the movie.

A helpful question to ask yourself is, "If I hold onto this hurt, what will my life look like years from now?" Scripture talks about pursuing wisdom in our lives. A wise thing to do is to press play and think ahead to where unforgiveness could lead. I have yet to meet a person who said, "Man, I am so thankful that I held onto this offense. It has led to job promotions. I am the healthiest I have ever been, and I am just so full of love for God and others." In fact, I have heard just the opposite: "I can't believe what this has done to my life and how it has ruined me. I lost my marriage. I lost my kids. I can't sleep at night, and this has destroyed everything that carried any meaning and value in my life." It can all be traced back to roots of unforgiveness. If you press play on the movie, you will quickly realize that the end of unforgiveness is misery. However, when you view it from that perspective, you will be empowered to move forward in the way of forgiveness.

4. Ask for God's help in the process.

The enemy wants you to stay trapped in offense and unforgiveness, but Christ's power is at work within you, which means you are not alone in the process of forgiveness. I intentionally use the word "process" here because forgiveness is truly a process. Forgiveness isn't always a one-and-done act. You will likely have to rely on Christ's power to overcome and forgive the offender.

Jesus says that the Holy Spirit empowers us to be witnesses for Him. A witness does more than speak about something. Being a witness for Christ is a lifestyle. He didn't leave us as orphans. Jesus sent His Holy Spirit to enable us to live fully alive in Him. So, why attempt to forgive on your own? Why not let Christ empower you to choose to respond with forgiveness? We serve a King who can empathize with us, who knows what we need before we ever ask Him. It makes sense to seek His help in the process of forgiveness. We must continually acknowledge Him and His power in our lives in order to experience the transformation He wants to bring.

5. Release full justice into the hands of Jesus.

When someone treats us poorly, we love to try to control the situation and take justice into our own hands. At the end of the day, it's possible that your accuser could get off the hook, go free, and you never see justice, which could be a hard pill to swallow. What do we do? Let's remember who will judge everyone according to how they lived their lives and who has the final say. Each of us will have to give an account for every action we took on Earth.

Nothing is hidden from Christ's sight, but the fullness of justice is found in His death and resurrection. In Malachi 3, we see the Israelites screaming and crying out for justice, asking when God will show up on their behalf. His response came in the form of the promised Messiah, Jesus Christ, who would fulfill a new covenant and bring a new kingdom to the earth. We are given a full picture of justice through Jesus' execution when He took the sin of the entire world upon Himself. The justice the Israelites were looking for is found in Jesus. God's wrath was on display when Christ took up the cross for you and me. The hurt and injustice we experience has already been dealt with on the cross. We can sleep at night knowing Jesus was and is enough. Because of Him, we can let go and trust God and His plan for our lives. We can surrender our fears, worries, and offenses back over to Him.

6. How can this offense help others overcome?

One way to heal is to discover how the offense you experienced plays into a greater narrative for someone else's healing. More than likely, hundreds of people have also experienced what you've gone through. God often uses our mess as a message of hope for others. While what happened to you isn't meant to become your identity, when in Christ's hands, it can be used for good in someone else's life. One of the most beautiful demonstrations of the gospel is the new purpose Christ gives those He encounters. Whether it was the tax collector, woman with the issue of blood, or the demoniac man, Christ had a way of reaching the vulnerable, healing them, and sending them out to share their story—and He is still moving. Your story could be a catalyst for the healing work of Christ in another person's life. How might God want to use your story of offense to help heal others? Discovering the answer will help you view your pain from Christ's perspective and as a part of His overall purpose. Remember, there isn't anything that He can't redeem. He is the great restorer!

7. Pray for those who hurt you.

Christ's instruction to pray for our enemies is one of the hardest instructions to follow. I'm sure many of us cringe on the inside when we read that passage of Scripture, but we aren't called to pray only for people who think and act just like us. We are called to pray for our enemies and bless those who mistreat us. This is the message of the gospel, the way of Christ. When we pray in His power and bless and forgive those who hurt us, we demonstrate His supernatural love and empowerment. The love of Christ is what heals and covers a multitude of sins, and it helps us see and treat others the way Christ would.

Jesus, the gospel, and His message of forgiveness are foolish things in the world's eyes. There is a veil between them and God, keeping them from receiving His truth and the fullness of life. Even so, as followers of Christ, we do not have permission to respond foolishly to their actions. We may be ridiculed for forgiving and loving those who cause us pain, but even Jesus forgave those who persecuted and hung Him on a tree to die. There is no sin that Christ did not forgive. Love and a life full of the Holy Spirit compelled Him. We, too, have the Holy Spirit, who came to help us live like Jesus.

Chapter 10

The Key to Freedom

"Finally, brothers and sisters, whatever is
true, whatever is noble, whatever is right, whatever is
pure, whatever is lovely, whatever is admirable—if
anything is excellent or praiseworthy—think about such
things." — Philippians 4:8

The key to freedom will always be Jesus.

Before Jesus started His public ministry, the Holy Spirit
led Him into the wilderness to be tested by the same
enemy who overpowered Adam and Eve. When Christ
was fasting and praying for forty days, the enemy came
and tried to tempt Him. How did Jesus overcome
temptation when He came face-to-face with the father
of lies? Each time the enemy tried to attack His identity
as the Son of God, Jesus masterfully gave a crucial
response to the devil's tactics. Jesus responded with the
Word of God. Through this testing, Jesus gave us the
prime example of how we, too, can overcome the

enemy's lies and temptations. He shows us that the key to freedom and living a life above the grave is His Word. The Word is enough. According to John 1, Jesus is the Word, and the Word is the only tool we need to achieve victory over the lies and strongholds of the enemy. Jesus didn't bow down to the lies and temptations thrown His way. He responded to the enemy with Scripture every time.

We have more access to the Bible now than at any point and time in history. Bibles are available in hotel rooms, and we even have the Bible app. The Bible is everywhere; however, although we have access to God's Word, we treat it as meaningless and useless. As the generation after us grows, they are becoming more and more biblically illiterate. If a generation becomes illiterate to God's Word, then it's possible that we could lose the fight when it comes to living fully alive in Jesus.

I find it interesting that the very first psalm shows us the key to winning in Christ. It tells us that it's possible to bear fruit in each and every season, and that the way to do that is to meditate on the Word of God day and night. It says that we are like trees that prosper, and our leaves do not wither because we are rooted in God's

Word.

Jesus said very plainly that those who obey what He says will be blessed. The Bible is full of instruction, insight, and encouragement. It is the weapon we use to guard ourselves from the enemy and live victoriously. If Jesus used Scripture to combat Satan, then we MUST use Scripture to help us stand firm in the Lord. In Ephesians 6, the apostle Paul describes Scripture, the Word of God, as the sword of the Spirit. When a warrior gets a sword, he or she doesn't carry the sword around simply for people to look at it. The sword is intentionally used offensively to bring forth victory. The Word was never meant to merely be heard. It is meant to be used on the offense—to be memorized and on the edge of our lips, ready to quote in response to the enemy.

The Word is not only a weapon; it's also a filter. As followers of Jesus, we need to filter everything through the Word of God. If something lines up with His Word, then we are good to go. If something contradicts God's Word, then we should have nothing to do with it. Could it be that we value our feelings and ideologies over the God-breathed and inspired written Word of God? Could it be that we are overtly subjective because we do not currently stand on the Word? There is only one lens we should look through, and it's the Bible.

I am all in on God's Word. It is intended for correction, teaching, and so much more. It is my guide and my key to freedom. Let me be clear. Only the blood of Jesus can wipe away every sin. Only Jesus can save, but my weapon in response to Satan's lies and temptation is the same one Jesus used. Since He used Scripture to fight, I will, too. What is it about the Word of God that gives us victory? The simple and plain answer is this: Scripture is TRUTH. John tells us that the truth sets us free, and whom the Son sets free is free indeed.

Not only is the Word of God our weapon, but the Holy Spirit, who now lives and dwells inside of us, leads us into all truth. I love how the Holy Spirit partners with the Word of God and utilizes it to help us fight and live life above the grave. I regularly ask students, "How can the Holy Spirit remind you of the truth if you don't open your Bible and have a hunger for His Word?" The Spirit works in conjunction with the Word of God. When we take time to study His Word and meditate on it, the Holy Spirit amplifies it throughout our day.

God frequently speaks to me when I'm reading Scripture during my quiet time. One of my regular routines is to read one chapter in the book of Psalms, one chapter in Proverbs, and one chapter in one of the four Gospels. I thoroughly enjoy reading Psalms because it connects with the emotional side of how God made me, and it is brutally honest in its poetry. I love the book of Proverbs, because it is so practical with its everyday wisdom and advice. I also love reading something from the Gospels each day, because I want to continually be reminded of the model Jesus set through His life and the words He spoke. Before bed every so often, I read the letters Paul wrote. I simply can't emphasize the power of Scripture enough.

I want to end this chapter with a story that helps illustrate the power of God's truth and of applying His Word in our lives. I love my wife more than anyone on this planet. Steph and I met at North Central University in downtown Minneapolis. It was love at first sight for me. I remember thinking that there was no way a guy like me could end up with a girl like her. She is beautiful, and I am not. She is smart, and I am not. She is organized, and I am not. She can sing like an angel, and I cannot. I could keep going with this list, but the point is that God hooked a brother up! My life hasn't been the same since marrying her. She challenges me in so many ways.

I remember a time in college when I was dropping her off after a date on a beautiful summer night. We'd enjoyed our time together, and before she got out of the car she said, "Micah, I need to tell you something." She got really quiet and didn't speak for a long while. I noticed that she began to shake, and her voice quivered as she started to speak. Whatever she was about to tell me, I knew she was nervous and unsure of what my response would be. She began to tell me about an ongoing battle with an eating disorder, one that had consumed her life for many years. Tears started to flow, and she didn't stop shaking. After she finished sharing, I placed my hand on her back and told her that this didn't define her. She told me later that she'd expected me to push her away and want nothing to do with her. She wasn't expecting grace and mercy, because not everyone in her life had responded that way. She'd been told that she needed to pray or read her Bible more, which all came from pure-hearted and well-intentioned people. However, their responses led to an internal belief that she was wrong and that it was due to an inability to spend time with Jesus.

For the next several years, I had the honor and privilege of walking alongside the woman who would become my wife. I wasn't about to let sin get the final word about who she was. I was going to attempt to love her the way Christ does. Last time I checked, the Bible says that Christ's love is patient, kind, gentle, doesn't envy, isn't proud, doesn't dishonor others, isn't self-seeking, KEEPS NO RECORD OF WRONGS, always protects, always trusts, always hopes, always perseveres, and NEVER FAILS. That was my call and my response moving forward. I can't change her or anyone else. I can't save anyone, so I couldn't approach her with a savior mentality. All I could do was love her like Jesus. I think all of us would be better off remembering that. LOVE LIKE JESUS.

Emphasizing my response isn't the point of this story. I am sharing it to show you the power of God's Word and revelation in our lives. My wife happened to attend a retreat where she heard a speaker challenge every woman to write down the lies they believed about themselves. For the next several minutes, she did just that. Then the speaker said, "Now I want you to write down every truth from God's Word over every lie." As my wife did this, she began to cry as she realized the stark differences between the lies and the truth. God's truth began to take root and overtake the lies that gripped her mind and heart. She began to read, meditate on, and speak the truth of God's Word over her life daily. It transformed her and released her to receive the truest thing about her—that she is a daughter of the King and every lie had to bow to His Word.

My wife's pathway to freedom didn't involve a motivational speech. Her healing and freedom came when she believed the truth of God's Word. She has been set free from that addiction ever since, and she presses forward past the feelings, past the lies, and into His truth. What she experienced wasn't just for her. Millions of people around the world also get to experience it when they open their Bibles and receive the truth of who they are in Christ. The key to freedom is Christ in you and His Word revealed.

Chapter 11

What Is the Wise Thing to Do?

It was the last day in the office for the overseer of the family ministry. I'd previously gotten to youth pastor alongside him, and he'd become one of my best friends. Whenever it was someone's last day, the lead pastor would give the staff an opportunity to say their goodbyes and parting words of encouragement. There were about twenty of us there to send him off, and each person shared how much they loved being around him and how he'd helped move the church forward. One word I kept hearing people say was "wise." Nearly everyone mentioned the wisdom he spoke and led with. I could always go to his office and receive sound feedback or advice. One thing was for sure: Wisdom marked his life.

At the end of the gathering, my friend spoke up to say his goodbyes and how encouraged he was to hear that we thought he was wise beyond his years. He shared that he'd made it a daily practice to pursue wisdom. He said, "Nearly every day for the past year I have been asking God to fill me and give me His wisdom." Did you catch it? He took time out of his day every day, to ask God to give him His wisdom. In Scripture, James writes about how we can ask God to give us wisdom and expect Him to give it to us. I love that God dedicated entire chapters of the Bible to reveal His wisdom and offer practical help and guidance for a life above the grave.

I love how God loves and teaches us. As a father, one of my desires is to see my own children succeed and live fully alive. I want to do everything I can to help my children grow into Godliness and wisdom. I want them to know there is a different way than what the world presents, and it's found in applying the wisdom and instruction in God's Word. His instruction is pure, flawless and life-giving. The Gospel of John tells us that God will not leave us as orphans but has given us an advocate, the Holy Spirit. Before Jesus left the earth, He equipped the disciples for life above the grave. One of the ways He equips us is through what He speaks in His Word. The book of Proverbs is a reminder of God's faithfulness in His desire to lead me, empower me, and help build my life.

There are 31 chapters in Proverbs, and it was originally written for young boys in the Jewish community. They were told to devote their lives to the wisdom found within the book and to never let it go. The instruction found in Proverbs is worth more than what money can buy, and it's often read by business leaders all over the world, including those who don't believe in Jesus. The truths in it have literally saved people from unnecessary evil and cruelty. You cannot read a chapter and not walk away feeling convicted by God or reminded of truth.

When I read Proverbs, I don't see a bunch of rules or obligations. I see a heavenly Father who wants to instruct His children in the way they should go. I hear a Father's love for His kids. There's one thing you should take note of, though. Whenever you read the Old Testament, read it through the lens of the Gospel of Jesus Christ. If you don't read the Old Testament from the perspective of Jesus and His saving grace, you may easily fall into a "works" based theology. Jesus came to replace the old covenant, to issue a new covenant based upon His works alone. We could interpret that our own purity and works are enough for God's favor; however, we see in the New Testament that our own righteousness is like filthy rags. Christ's righteousness is bestowed upon us through our faith in Him. The wisdom

Jesus gives helps us ditch the grave clothes and walk into the good works He has prepared in advance for our lives. It's His wisdom that allows us to walk in purity and integrity.

Every car has a dashboard with built in lights, like the "check engine" or "low oil" light, that notify the driver when there is a problem somewhere within the car. In the same way, the book of Proverbs has a way of flashing lights in our lives, alerting us when we may be heading down the wrong path. We all need daily inspections in our pursuit of Jesus. Proverbs will help us check our hearts as we walk with Him through life.

One of the day-to-day disciplines I have tried to consistently implement is reading a chapter of Proverbs every day. I take time to read each one slowly and allow it to touch my heart and mind. Some months in a calendar year have thirty-one days, which can help you stay on track with reading a chapter of Proverbs a day. For example, today is August 3, so I read Proverbs 3. I encourage you to give it a try. I'm convinced that if we apply God's Word and ask for His wisdom and understanding, it will transform our days. I consider myself blessed to have so many wise friends and mentors. The common denominator is their pursuit of Jesus, His wisdom, and His instruction. They are people I've watched pray and study the scriptures for insight. Their lives are marked by humility, generosity, honor, and total dependency on Jesus. While they aren't perfect, they recognize their need to pursue Him daily.

I've now lived several years without a father. When I think of the role of a father in a child's life, I think of someone who oversees and offers wisdom and guidance, which is something that's been missing in my life for a while. I often feel very inadequate when it comes to certain things in life, and I find myself longing to pick up the phone to talk to my dad and ask him basic, everyday questions. The comfort a dad can bring and the wisdom he can share are incredibly valuable. I think about that from time-to-time and end up feeling like I'm missing out. I want to clarify that this doesn't mean that moms are not wise. Believe me, my mom is filled with incredible insight and I often consult her. However, I feel an intense void when it comes to not having a father. But I've seen God's faithfulness through the people He has placed around me and the relationships I have with them. I think of how many times I had my mind made up about a particular plan, only to have it halted because someone wiser stepped in and course-corrected me. In His faithfulness, God gives us wisdom through people.

Wisdom isn't something you drift into; it has to be intentionally built into your life. Here are some practical ways to get God's wisdom every day.

1. Read a chapter of Proverbs each day.

I already mentioned how you can apply this each and every day. It doesn't take long, and it could save you from a lifetime of misery.

2. Pray and ask for God's wisdom every day.

I mentioned that a friend of mine prayed and asked for God's wisdom daily. This simple act made him wise beyond his years, and he still pursues wisdom every day. Remember, when you ask for God's wisdom, expect to receive it.

3. Become a lifelong learner.

Everyone has the opportunity to grow right where they are. Proverbs tells us to incline our hearts toward knowledge and instruction. We are called to do whatever we can to get insight and understanding. There are countless ways to grow right where you are. Books are a great way to learn and develop. My goal is to read a minimum of 30 books each year to sharpen me and help me keep growing.

You can also get a mentor, and he or she doesn't have to be local. You can be mentored by leaders all over the world. Podcasts are a great place to start. I have a goal of listening to 104 podcasts each year. I listen to people who are wiser than me. I desire to to live a life above the grave and grow in wisdom, not to stay where I am. Craig Groeschel, Andy Stanley, Ravi Zacharias, Carey Neiuwhof, and John Lindell are just a few who have mentored me from afar. I've never sat down to have lunch with them. Although I would love that, I can simply go to a coffee shop to listen and begin applying their teaching in my life.

I also gain a lot of insight from older, more seasoned

ministers and other local mentors. Once a month, I meet with my pastor to check in. I can confidently say that a big reason I'm where I am today is because of other leaders who went before me and helped pave the way for me. One of those leaders is a man by the name of Jerry Strandquist. Pastor Jerry has the gift of seeing leadership in young people, developing them, then sending them out to go lead other endeavors. He has an ability to see things in others that they may not see themselves. Jerry is one of those guys who took a chance on me and gave me my first-ever ministry position at a church. He gave me room to fall, bruise, skin my knee, and helped me get back up again and begin the healing process. He gave me space and grace to grow into the man and leader God was calling me to become. I honor him, his leadership, and how God used him to develop and challenge me. I say all of this to say that having older and wiser mentors in our lives to watch, study and learn from is invaluable. And the good news is that anybody can do what I listed above to get wisdom and apply it to their lives.

Pastor Andy Stanley once proposed a great question we can all ask ourselves: "What is the wise thing to do?" I love this question, because every day is filled with choices. A simple question like that can spare us unnecessary pain. What is the wise thing to do? If I go ahead and make this decision, how will it impact me and others around me? If you don't know the answer, that's a good indication that you should reach out to others who are wiser than you. I've realized that allowing the right people to speak into my decisions allows me to gain a perspective that I didn't have but that I needed.

REMEMBER THIS: God is for you and not against you. He is with you and will never forsake you. However, by offering His wisdom, He has given you everything you need to live life above the grave. But we're not done yet. Let's take a look at another way He equips us to live in His freedom.

Chapter 12

Prayer and Fasting

At the end of his life, a minister was reflecting on his life and ministry and said, "As a minister, I spent about two-thirds of my time studying Scripture and one-third of my time praying. If I could do it all over again, I would spend two-thirds of my time praying and one-third of my time studying Scripture." His name was Leonard Ravenhill, and God used him mightily in teaching the subject of prayer. *Revival Praying* is a great book of his that I highly recommend.

Prayer is often something a follower of Jesus neglects first. In contrast, Jesus' disciples asked Him to teach them how to pray. Why wouldn't they ask Him how to preach better sermons, cast out more demons, or walk on water? Why did they ask Jesus to teach them how to pray? I think what the disciples saw Jesus doing more than anything else wasn't miracles or preaching. I think they remembered all the morning they'd woken up and couldn't find Jesus because He'd gone to be alone and spend time praying with His Father in heaven.

Jesus didn't just spend time praying. He spent time praying and fasting. If Jesus, the Son of God, spent His life praying and fasting, how much more do you and I need to pray and fast? Jesus came to show us what it meant to live out the new kingdom He was bringing forth. Prayerlessness quickly leads to powerlessness. A prayer-filled life is a power-filled life. It is extremely difficult to sin when you are praying and crying out to Jesus.

At some point, I'll write a book on prayer, because we'll need more than just one chapter to talk about its power. However, this chapter will equip you to live a life of freedom above the grave, and it will help you understand how God builds His kingdom on earth through our prayers. So, let's talk about seven practical steps to help you live a life of prayer and fasting.

1. The blood of Jesus washes and cleanses us from sin.

As you read the first point, you might be scratching your head and thinking, "I thought this was about prayer and fasting." This has everything to do with prayer and fasting! It's crucial to remember that your good works aren't what save or cleanse you. You cannot manipulate God into making you more holy or righteous because you prayed for an hour today. There's only one thing that can save you, wash you clean, and make you as white as snow—the blood of Jesus that was shed on a cross for you and me.

The Pharisees questioned Jesus about why His disciples didn't fast. The Pharisees loved making themselves seem strong outwardly, but they were spiritually bankrupt inwardly and needed their hearts to be cleansed and washed. On the outside, they looked like they did everything right. But on the inside, they were lost and broken just like their neighbors. Jesus came to transform the heart, which is deceitful and wicked, not to bring outward perfection. He came to bring us His righteousness that we could never attain on our own, which is why I started with this point. We get to rejoice every morning that we are covered in His blood and righteousness. We get to delight in His goodness. We can smile and begin each day in Jesus' love and grace. When we pray and fast, we get to start with a posture of gratitude and freedom, because we never have to earn our place or our purity with Him. THAT RIGHT THERE

DESERVES A GIANT CLAP TO JESUS. GO AHEAD. PUT THE BOOK DOWN, TELL HIM THANKS, AND GIVE HIM A CLAP OF PRAISE!

2. Find a place you can go to pray every day. (Hint: If you apply it, this may be the greatest takeaway from the entire book.)

Most of the time, we don't pray because we aren't intentional about it. Prayer can become a part of our routines when we're purposeful about scheduling it. I don't want to bind you to a certain method or timeframe, because each of us is different. I, personally, devote my mornings to prayer, because I want to give God the first part of my day. Throughout Scripture, there are principles of "firsts." We are called to seek first His kingdom. We are called to give our firstfruits. We are called to first forgive others before bringing a sacrifice of worship to God. There's something special about our "firsts."

One of the things I love challenging students and others to do is to create a prayer room at home where they can spend time with Jesus every day. I get to challenge students all across the world to create these rooms and to take some things with them. If you decide to create a space of your own, make sure to bring a Bible, a notebook or journal, and a list of friends and people who need Jesus and breakthrough. I also recommend a playlist to set the atmosphere with praise and worship. Your prayer room can be a closet, your bedroom or wherever else you can go to be alone with God. Having a set place to pray and spend time with Jesus can change your whole day, and a changed day can lead to a changed life. You guys, it really is a lot of fun! Nothing has changed my life more than the grace and love of Jesus and finding a place to pray and spend time in His presence.

3. The more you pray, the more you will pray.

Have you ever seen a child trying to ride a bike for the first time? They are shaky and wobbly, and it's nerve racking to watch. I can imagine one of the reasons why so few people pray or enjoy prayer is that they don't know how or what to pray. So, it seems pointless or ineffective. What I've found to be true in my own life is the more I pray and spend time with Jesus, the more I want to pray and spend time with Him. It's kind of like an appetite. If all you do is eat fast food and Taco Bell goodness, your tastebuds crave more of it. By the way, my go-to order at Taco Bell is a number seven with no jalapeño sauce and rather than a crunchy shell, I enjoy a soft shell instead. I also get the best soda they have, which is their Baja Blast. (Don't @ me.) Those late-night cravings become my consistent reality if all I do is consume those kinds of foods. The same is true when I spend time with Jesus in the same place regularly. (Sidenote: Don't be afraid to change the scenery and mix up where you go to spend time in His presence.) The more I do that, the more I long to talk to Him and keep the conversation going throughout the day, which leads to my next point.

4. Keep the conversation going with God.

Prayer isn't a one-and-done thing. It isn't something to just add a checkmark next to so we can say we fulfilled our religious duty for the day. Prayer is an ongoing conversation. Remember, God doesn't dwell in a building; He dwells within YOU. Wherever you go, He goes, too. Life is way more fun when you acknowledge God throughout your day and not just in the morning. I consistently find myself telling Jesus how much I love Him and how grateful I am for Him.

I also find myself thanking Him for ordering my steps and leading me to whomever and wherever I go during the day. One of the most rewarding things about being in relationship with Jesus is how specific and encouraging He is. For example, I took my kids to the park the other day. I typically sit on a bench and watch them play. This time something different happened. I felt the Holy Spirit speak to me and say, "Micah, go over by your son. He's about to fall." When I looked at him, he was climbing up an arched ladder and was nearing the top almost eight feet off the ground. He looked stable to me and only had a few steps left, but I decided to walk over to him anyway. Just as he was about to take his last step, he slipped. He would have fallen eight feet down to the ground, but I was right there to catch him. The look on his face was one of utter terror, but he was quickly comforted when I caught him. This kind of thing isn't an uncommon occurrence for me. I often hear God's voice speaking to me, and it makes me think about how good, timely, and relational He is toward us.

Prayer isn't a monologue. It's a dialogue with the creator of the universe. You could potentially have several meetings with people on any given day. I promise you, there is no greater meeting than with the one who made you and knit you together in your mother's womb.

Prayer is a two-way street, so, whenever you pray, make sure you stop to listen for His voice in return. Write down what you sense He is saying. He's so faithful to us.

5. Pray with expectation.

When we pray and ask God for something, we can trust that He will answer. In His Word, Jesus says that we do not have because we do not ask. We can ask anything in Jesus' name and expect to see God move. This isn't an opportunity to ask for lottery wins or new houses and cars. Prayer is an opportunity for us to partner with the will of God. We can ask God to show up in ways that align with His character and heart. I often pray for those who need a miracle or healing. I pray that my friends who don't know Christ will encounter His presence and His love. I pray blessing and unity over my own church and the pastors I serve underneath. I pray Scripture over my family and others in my life. I pray for governing authorities and those God has placed and appointed in positions of authority.

If you don't know what to pray or what to ask for, a great place to start is by opening your Bible. Praying God's Word is praying in agreement with what He has already spoken. One passage of Scripture that I pray most is John 17. In it, we see Jesus praying over His disciples, and there are a couple of themes that I pray over myself and others. Jesus prayed for protection from the evil one. He prayed that His disciples would be sanctified in the truth and forever growing in Him. Then He prayed that they would be one and unified.

So, here are three powerful themes you can also pray over yourself:

a. protection from Satan and his schemes
b. that we would grow to be like Christ in His truth
c. that we would do everything to be unified

I love how Scripture gives us models for prayer. The Lord's Prayer is another one we can follow. In Matthew 6, Jesus taught His disciples to pray this way and showed us how to begin and end in prayer. It sounds too simple to be true but, many times, we don't see certain things fulfilled in our lives because we don't ask. We need to get back to asking Jesus for things based upon His will.

6. Make a list.

This is very practical. Make a list of people who need a breakthrough or healing. Make a list of people who are lost and need to be found. This will help you stay focused and organized in your prayer time and bring things God has called you to pray for back to mind.

I have three different categories that help me stay focused when I pray. I start my prayer time with worship and thanksgiving. I give God praise and thank Him for who He is in my life, then I shift my prayer to the three categories:

a. Breakthrough: I pray for people who have a dire need and who are hurting or recovering medically. I pray for people who are lost and don't know Jesus. I pray for those battling addictions. I pray that the veil that covers their eyes would be removed and that they would clearly see the truth of the gospel. I pray that Jesus would set free those who need breakthrough.

b. Spiritual insight to defeat the enemy: I ask God to give me spiritual insight in defeating the enemy. I ask Him to show me where the enemy might try to attack or where he might try to tempt me. I ask God for His insight so I can be on guard and stand firm in Him. I also take time to pray the full armor of God, which you can find in Ephesians 6 if you'd like to pray it over yourself.

c. I pray blessing and God's favor over my family, ministry and others. I don't start off praying for myself. Instead, I pray for other evangelists and pastors who run ministries like ours. I pray for God's favor and the windows of heaven to be opened up over them and their ministries. Jealousy and greed like to sneak in when we don't pray blessing over others. I text my friends and let them know I am genuinely praying for their schedules and calendars to be full and for God to bless their ministries. As I've prayed for other ministries, I've seen God's favor come over ours. I'm not saying we have the magic formula, but God does command blessing where there is unity. Keep disunity far away from your heart, and value God and His unity.

7. Check off the list.

Checking names off the list is one of my favorite things to do. Just recently, two friends I've been praying would come to Christ gave their lives to Him. I was able to cross their names off the list as I watched God do a work in their hearts. I literally broke down and cried. When you pray and agree with God, He is faithful.

While checking things off the list has been incredibly rewarding, I've also experienced disappointment throughout my prayer journey. What happens when you pray and ask Jesus, but you experience the exact opposite of what you prayed? What happens when you pray and don't see the miracle? I have seen this plenty of times in my own life, but let me encourage you with a story about how good God is to help illustrate what I'm trying to tell you.

My dad met Rich over twenty years ago. He's the mechanic our family has been taking our cars to ever since. Dad always prayed that Rich would come to know Christ. Anytime my dad would talk about Jesus, Rich really didn't want anything to do with it. He'd end the conversation and move on to something else. Our family kept bringing him our cars whenever they needed to be worked on, and my mom often made him baked goods or popcorn so he had treats to enjoy at the shop. He always loved that.

When I dropped my car off this time, something was different. He stopped me and said, "Micah, would you keep me in your prayers?" I honestly thought it was a little strange. But he knew I was a minister, and I was curious as to what he wanted prayer for. He continued, "I have cancer and it's not looking good." I was heartbroken to hear the news. I said, "Rich, I am going to pray and fast for you every day until we see Jesus heal you." I believed for a total miracle and just knew it would lead to Rich's salvation. I prayed earnestly and sought Jesus on behalf of my friend. I was filled with so much faith and expectation, and I was convinced we were going to witness the supernatural.

A couple of months passed, and the cancer had gotten worse, so Rich was placed in the hospital. He was draining a liter of fluids from his lungs every day, and it was getting bad. As my buddy and I were about to leave the hospital room after our visit one day, Rich stopped us and said, "Hey, I had a Mormon guy stop by the other day. He prayed for me and did this weird oil thing. What do you guys think about all of that stuff?" I realized what Rich was trying to get at. He was wondering what would happen to his soul if he died. We sat down on either side of his bed and I said, "Rich, I can't tell you much about

Mormonism, but one thing I can tell you about is Jesus and His Good News for you and me." I began to explain the love Jesus has for him, and he started to sob in his hospital bed. When I finished sharing, I said, "Rich, would you like to receive Christ as your Lord and Savior?" That day we got to lead our mechanic to Jesus. After we prayed with him to receive Jesus, Rich let out a big breath of air and said, "That was the most glorious moment of my life." I am convinced that Rich encountered a mercy and grace he had never experienced before. He could be at peace and rest knowing His soul was in the hands of His creator. Just a few days later, Rich breathed his last breath on the earth.

I'd prayed and had so much faith for a miracle, but I realized that I'd actually witnessed the greatest miracle anyone could witness. I got to see Jesus transform my friend's heart. I selfishly want Rich to be alive and well today, and I believed he would be. However, God had a different plan. What's so amazing is that I had the honor of leading Rich's funeral service and watching as a couple hundred of Rich's friends heard the same Good News that he did before he died. A prayer in faith for physical healing is where it all started, but it ended up being multiplied and reaching hundreds of people.

Most of the time, I don't understand God and His ways, but I trust Him with all my heart and lean not on my own understanding. I pray for His will to be done and His kingdom to come. That day I got to check my friend Rich off the list, and I can't wait to see him again in heaven.

Chapter 13

The Holy Spirit

I used to work at Best Buy. It was the best. Get it? "Best." Ha ha. Anyway, I sincerely loved my job and the people I got to work with. To this day I am still friends with some of my old coworkers. The discount was also amazing. I bought subwoofers and a nice sound system, so my car was the loudest on the block. I was "that guy" in the neighborhood who you could hear coming from a mile away. I was always bumping that Jesus music, mostly Lecrae. While Best Buy had its perks, the most impactful part of working there wasn't the sales or experiences; it was the one who lives inside of me. I know that sentence may sound weird, but it's easy for a lot of us to forget that the God of the universe lives inside of those who believe and follow Jesus. Just hang with me here and you'll see where I'm going with this.

Many of us associate spirituality with certain places or buildings. I can totally understand that, but we must not forget that God never wanted to be confined to buildings. Man has this fascination with places to house or store things, and there was a thought that if we built temples or churches, God would come and be pleased. However, Scripture constantly shows us that the God of the Bible cannot and will not be contained. The temple was sacred. It was considered to be a place where heaven and earth collided, the point of intersection between the two. The temple was a place where God dwelled and where a priest could access Him on behalf of the people. However, in the New Testament we see a radical shift in God's plan and desire.

When the virgin Mary gave birth to Jesus, He was given the name Emmanuel, which means "GOD WITH US." From the very start of Jesus' life, He was communicating that God is here with us, and He'd be with us even after He died. Prior to His death, He told the disciples that it was better for Him to leave the earth because someone named the Holy Spirit was going to come. (By the way, John 14-16 are great reference points for Jesus' teaching on the coming of the Holy Spirit.) Jesus was bringing forth something NEW, and it involved the Holy Spirit coming to dwell within man. The temple was no longer going to be a building; the people were going to become the temple. God was going to take up residence within us. The Gospel of John tells us that the Holy Spirit was on His way to lead us into all truth.

It's important to understand that the Holy Spirit isn't a ghost or some creepy alien-like figure floating around. The Holy Spirit is not an "IT." The Holy Spirit is the person of God. You see, we have God the Father, God the Son, and God the Holy Spirit. All three are active in Scripture, but we see the emphasis of the Holy Spirit after Jesus leaves.

I want to do a quick teaching on the role of the Holy Spirit in our lives based upon the words of Jesus in the Gospel of John.

1. The Holy Spirit is our advocate. — John 14:16

I love that the first word used to describe the Spirit is "advocate", someone who fights for us and stands up for us. There's a stark contrast between the enemy being described as an "accuser of the brethren" and the Holy Spirit's characterization as our "advocate." I think it's a beautiful explanation of the Holy Spirit's role in our lives.

2. The Holy Spirit lives with us and dwells in us. —
John 14:17

You can't get much clearer than this statement. God
now lives inside of us. You might be thinking, "How can
He live inside of me when I feel like such a terrible
person all the time?" Well, there is an internal war
between your flesh and your spirit. The apostle Paul
wrote about the war within every believer. You can
choose to either gratify the desires of your flesh, which
are sinful and lead to death and destruction. Or you can
choose to gratify the desires of the Spirit, the God who
lives inside you, which leads to everlasting life. The fact
that you sense the internal fight to rid your life of sin is
evidence of the Holy Spirit, who wants to make you holy,
living inside of you.

When we were born, we already knew how to sin. We
were born with an appetite for things that are contrary
to God's plan for our lives. We have a sinful nature, but
when we choose to surrender and follow Jesus, He gives
us His Holy Spirit, who helps us become more like Christ.
As you can imagine, becoming like Him is not an
overnight process. The Holy Spirit will continue to make
you more and more like Him for the remainder of your
life.

3. The Holy Spirit is a teacher and reminds us of the truth. — John 14:26

Not only is the Holy Spirit an advocate, He's also a teacher. He will never leave us or forsake us. Instead, He comes to teach us and remind us of the truth throughout our lives. And I just want to say that it's hard to remind people of the truth when they have no desire to hear or read it. The Holy Spirit is God and can do whatever He pleases. However, we are in partnership with Him.

As I go through each day, the Holy Spirit frequently reminds me of things I've read in His Word. Every one of us needs the Word of God, and we should all make time to read it daily, because God speaks truth through His Word. The Holy Spirit can only remind us of the truth if we know what God's Word says. Why do we need to be reminded of the truth? Because we so often forget it and, if we aren't careful, we can begin to exchange the truth about God for a lie. Romans 1 shows us how vile the wicked heart of man can become. It shows us how the people were destroyed when they chose to exchange the truth for a lie and God gave them over to the desires of their hearts.

Exchanging the truth for a lie is a scary place to be. Who is the instigator of lies? Satan, who is called "the father of lies." In the beginning, he deceived man and does the same even now. Our hearts are sinful, which is why we need the Holy Spirit to teach us and remind us of His truth. Without the Holy Spirit, we can find ourselves in some messy places.

4. The Holy Spirit will convict us of sin. — John 16:7-8

This may be one of my favorite things about the way the Holy Spirit functions inside of us. I am so grateful for His conviction in my life. I am notorious for not seeing and thinking properly, for wandering off every now and then. But the Holy Spirit is amazing at course-correcting and convicting me whenever I've grieved God.

Allow me to quickly explain conviction, because it can have a negative connotation. We live in a world where criminals are convicted and put into prison, so it's possible that we associate conviction with something bad. When we look at God, we realize that conviction isn't based on hate but rather on love. Conviction is rooted in love, while condemnation is rooted in hate. The Holy Spirit convicts and Satan condemns. There is a difference.

When I was a little boy, I played soccer with my dad in our side yard. When we were playing one day, the ball went into the street, and I took off after it. Just before I stepped into the street, I heard my father's voice yell, "MICAH, STOP!" As I stopped short of the road, a car came driving by. Had I not listened to my father, I would have gotten hit by the car because the driver couldn't see me coming, and my life could have ended. Conviction is a lot like our heavenly Father saying, "STOP, DON'T DO THIS. IT WILL DESTROY YOUR LIFE."

I pray often for the Holy Spirit's conviction. The book of Psalms instructs us to ask God to test and search our hearts to see if there is any offensive way within us. I once heard a pastor say, "Before I fall asleep each night, I ask God to convict me and show me where I was wrong today. I then ask for His forgiveness. I would rather be convicted each day than one day stand before my congregation and apologize for the hidden sin in my life." God sees things that we do not, and His conviction is necessary for us to live fully in Him.

5. The Holy Spirit will guide you into all truth. — John 16:13

We desperately need a guide in our daily lives, especially in the times we are currently living. The Holy Spirit offers discernment, which helps us sense when something is off, and works within us to lead us in the right direction. We live in a world of subjectivity and relativism, but subjective truth is no truth at all. God's truth is all truth, because God is truth. Like a good shepherd knows when and where to lead his sheep and looks out for threats, we have a God who seeks to order our steps, protect us, and guide us into His truth through the Holy Spirit.

6. The Holy Spirit will always glorify God. — John 16:14

The Holy Spirit doesn't dwell within us to bring us glory. He lives inside of us to bring glory to His name. I LOVE THIS SO MUCH. Our lives are not about us. They are all about Him and His glory. God is so good. He brings glory to His name through our lives and our testimonies. One of the tensions of living with the Holy Spirit is the temptation to receive glory for something God allowed to happen within you in order to impact others.

As a traveling minister, I meet thousands of people every year who think I "did something for them" or that I "helped save them." I know what they are trying to say, and I politely respond, "Thank you." But I know how spiritually bankrupt I am apart from Christ. I know full well that Christ is the one working through me, so I don't receive the praise from man. I know that pride can be quiet and deadly, and it can sneak into every one of our lives. Whenever I have those kinds of encounters with people after sharing a message, I tell them that God is the one who does the work. Then I thank Jesus that He was at work within their hearts. I give God the glory and honor.

I love Paul's response to the dispute between him and Apollos in 1 Corinthians 3. He describes himself as a bondservant of Jesus Christ. He knew his role when it came to following Jesus: SERVANT. We are all here as servants of Jesus, to reflect His glory in a dark world that needs His grace and light.

7. The Holy Spirit empowers you to be a witness. —
    Acts 1:8

Jesus told His disciples to wait in Jerusalem until the gift
of the Holy Spirit came. They obeyed and days later, as
they were meeting in an upper room praying and
worshipping God, the Holy Spirit fell and baptized all of
the believers there, and they began to speak in other
tongues. A man named Peter was the first person to
address the crowd. He was full of the Holy Spirit and
testified that Jesus is the promised Messiah. He called
those in attendance to repent and be baptized. That day
about 3,000 people came to Christ and began following
Him.

Jesus said, "You will receive power when the Holy Spirit
comes, and you will be my witnesses in Jerusalem,
Judea, Samaria, and to the ends of the earth." The
people were going to be empowered by the Holy Spirit
to be the witnesses Christ intended. This is SO
POWERFUL. We don't walk in our own power or grit.
When the Holy Spirit lives in us, He gives us His power to
live fully alive in Christ. The goal: BE A WITNESS.
Witnessing doesn't mean just using words. To witness to

the world around us, every one of us has to live a LIFESTYLE that demonstrates the gospel. That's what the Holy Spirit came to empower us to do. He was sent to help us live our lives above the grave. When you receive the Holy Spirit, He impacts every part of your life. He gives you power and boldness to live out the gospel.

One night after a staff party our store was hosting, some of my coworkers from Best Buy invited me to join them at a bar. I told them I would pass since I don't drink and that I would be calling it a night. On my drive home, with my Jesus music bumping loudly, I prayed that God would use me. I just simply said, "God, would you use me for your glory?" What happened next blew my mind.

I felt like I heard the Holy Spirit whisper back, "Go back to the bar and tell all of your employees about my love for them." As I felt my blood pressure rise, I turned my music up louder. I thought to myself, "There's no way God would want me to go do that." But I heard Him whisper again, "Go back. Go back." The Holy Spirit's voice got louder and louder each time. Once I finally got home, I got out of the car, shut the door, and started to make my way inside. Then I heard the whisper again.

When I walked through the front door, my sister was sitting there. She was the last person I wanted to see, because I knew she would challenge me to go back to the party. She could clearly see the distraught look on my face and asked, "Micah, what's wrong?" I responded, "I think God is telling me to go back to the bar and tell my coworkers about Jesus." Her reply: "Then you'd better get back in your car and go tell them about Jesus."

I remember crying and freaking out. While I was on my way back, I called one of my good friends, Brent Silkey, and told him what I was planning to do and how scared I was. He reassured me, "Micah, you will receive power when the Holy Spirit comes upon you." He reminded me that God is with me, that I'm filled with the Holy Spirit. As I walked into the bar, I motioned to the DJ to turn the music down so I could speak. I don't remember exactly what I said, but I do know that I couldn't stop talking about the love of Jesus and how much he loved everyone in that bar. Before I could finish, a coworker who was usually pretty quiet got up with tears in his eyes and reached out for a hug. I then noticed a line of people waiting to give me a hug and express how grateful they were to hear the gospel.

I left there knowing that I'd done what God told me to do. I'd asked Him to use me, and He answered. The Holy Spirit at work within me empowered me to be a witness that night. It was never about a moment in time. It was about allowing God to do what He wanted to do through me to bring glory to Himself. I don't know where I would be without the Holy Spirit living inside of me and empowering me to live for Jesus. I still fight an internal battle between flesh and spirit, but I know that God's Spirit in me is greater than anything I will face in this world.

I'm merely scratching the surface about who the Holy Spirit in this chapter. Maybe one day I'll write another book to share more, but I wanted to equip you with some knowledge about Him. I encourage you to read the book of Acts so you can see what a Spirit-filled life looks like. You'll notice that the people mentioned in Acts are often described as being "full of the Spirit." We were all designed to be full of the Holy Spirit and to live above the grave.

I also recommend further reading by Tim Enloe and Ty

Buckingham, who have each written phenomenal books about the Holy Spirit, who isn't just for one sect of people; He's for all tribes, tongues and nations.

Chapter 14

Go and Share

When I look back over the last 34 years of my life, I can't help smiling. I smile because of the faithfulness of God I've seen with my own eyes in such a short amount of time.

Naturally, when I get excited, I have to let everybody know what I'm excited about. I'm the guy who will probably find a way to get you excited about the new storm doors I just put on my house, or I'll try to convince you that living in Minnesota is the best.

It's normal to want to share something we're excited about. I'm overwhelmed with thanksgiving when I look back on where God has brought me from. I've had the honor of traveling and sharing my story with thousands across America and around the world. By the grace of God, I have witnessed thousands repent and believe in Jesus as Lord.

One of my utmost joys in following Jesus is the opportunity to share His love with others, whether in an auditorium full of young people or during an Uber ride back home from the airport. Everyone needs to know the Good News of Jesus Christ. When Jesus moves you from death to life, you're called to tell others about the life He's placed inside of you. Too many of us know what it means to be taken from death to life but never actually share what God has done. In the Bible, we see a common theme. The people who encountered Christ and were transformed were the same people who would go and tell others about the new life they'd been given.

In John 4, a Samaritan woman shares her testimony of meeting the Messiah. Because of her story, many believed. The demoniac man, who no one wanted to be around and who no one could subdue before He encountered the power of Jesus, became the first known evangelist in the Decapolis area. The Gospel of Mark describes how there were lines of people waiting for Jesus when He returned to the area. Before that, they had been terrified of Jesus and told Him to leave. Later, hundreds of people were awaiting His return. Why? Because the once naked, demoniac man was now dressed, and his life was restored back to order. The man obeyed Jesus when he was told to go and share his story. His obedience led to hundreds of people being set free, too. His life went from pain to purpose. Jesus has a way of doing that.

Before Jesus left, the disciples were tasked with the Great Commission, to go and preach the gospel and make disciples of all nations. Jesus' plan was to equip people to go and share their lives. Now more than ever we have the resources to go and share our stories with the world. The blood of Jesus and your testimony will help others overcome.

Recently, I shared a part of my story on TikTok and received many views from people in places like Indonesia, India, Japan, and Malaysia. It reached over 450,000 people with the message of the gospel. God works through our lives beyond what we can dream, ask for, or imagine. The Great Commission wasn't a suggestion or an opinion; it was a command. We are called to make disciples and share the love of Christ with those near and far.

This isn't a proven statistic, but I'm convinced that many

young people stop following Jesus because they've never actively shared their faith or experienced the beauty in seeing others impacted by Him. One of the greatest rewards in following Jesus is watching your friends start to follow Him or leading a co-worker to Him— when faith becomes real to them in a moment. We were meant to share what we have with the world around us. What we share isn't a better, more polished version of ourselves. Rather, we're called to share how broken and lost we were until Christ found us and made us alive in Him. We get to talk about the greatness and goodness of our God.

I wonder how excited we really are about God since so few of us ever actually talk about Him. We often discuss what we're passionate about, but I want to be found speaking about Christ more than anything else. I'm not here to be a pushy salesperson or force people to believe what I believe. I simply want my life to exude the glory of Christ and allow it to be a witness to the world. A life above the grave is a life that is laid down and spent on God's purposes. A life well spent is a life well shared. We often think a life well lived is all about how well we can receive, which couldn't be further from the truth. Jesus modeled this for us from the moment He came into the world and the moment He returned to His

Father in heaven. Jesus continuously laid His life down and offered up service to others.

I recently created a promo video for this book and sent it off to a friend to get his thoughts. The text message he sent in response said this: "Now I understand why you preach as hard as you do." There is a burning passion inside of me for everyone to know the love of Jesus. Christ has taken me from death to life. With the time I have left on Earth, I desire to make Him known and live life above the grave in pursuit of Him. I am far from perfect, but the goodness of Jesus is too good to keep to myself. It's easy to look at pastors and to default to them as the only authority in ministry or in sharing the gospel. However, God's plan was for YOU to be a minister of the gospel. Every one of us has good works to do throughout our lives. What story is God working in and through your life that will be used to encourage and build others up? What has God done in your life that wasn't meant for just you but was meant to help other people?

If you have never given your life to Jesus, I want to offer you an opportunity right now. Only Jesus can bring you from a place of death and into His everlasting life. Only

Jesus can save. He says, "I am the way, the truth, and the life." There is no way other than Jesus. Just as He found a hurting young man years ago and made me new, He can do the same for you. Allow me to lead you in a prayer of surrender to Jesus. You can pray this right where you are:

"Jesus, thank you for finding me. Thank you for loving me. I am lost and I need you. Would you forgive me of all my sin and cleanse me from the inside out? Jesus, I want to spend the rest of my life living for you. Thank you for saving and forgiving me. Help me to follow you all the days of my life. Thank you for giving me new life and purpose. Amen."

YOU ARE A NEW CREATION IN CHRIST JESUS! The old is gone and the new has come. He has brought you from death to life!

ABOUT THE AUTHOR

Micah MacDonald resides in Minnesota with his wife Stephanie Joy. Together, they lead a ministry called Mac Ministries. Mac Ministries gets to travel the world and preach the Gospel message of Jesus Christ. You can learn more about them by going to their website.

www.mac-ministries.com

If you would like to send them a message you can email:

Macmin@yahoo.com